The World According to

DANNY DYER

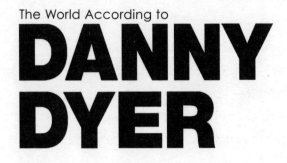

The World According to

DANNY DYER

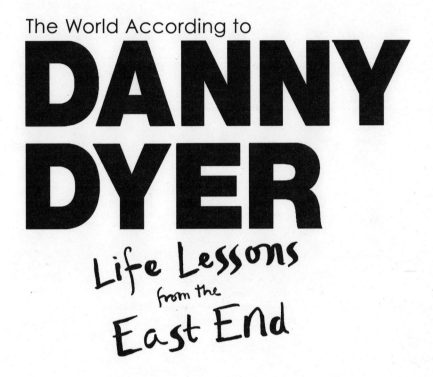

Life Lessons
from the
East End

Quercus

First published in Great Britain in 2015 by

Quercus Publishing Ltd
Carmelite House
50 Victoria Embankment
London EC4Y 0DZ

An Hachette UK company

A CIP catalogue record for this book is available
from the British Library

HB ISBN 978 1 78429 741 1
TPB ISBN 978 1 78429 788 6
EBOOK ISBN 978 1 78429 742 8

10 9 8 7 6 5 4 3 2 1

Typeset by Hewer Text UK Ltd, Edinburgh
Printed and bound in Great Britain by Clays Ltd, St Ives plc

'I think it is the responsibility of a citizen of any country to say what he thinks.'

Harold Pinter

To Jack and John, my two granddads,
who have both passed away.
Gone but never EVER forgotten.

Introduction

All right, me old chinas, it's me, Danny Dyer.

I suppose if you've bought this book you must know who I am. For a day job I play Mick Carter, landlord of The Queen Vic in *EastEnders*. It's a massive role, huge – and I don't say that to be big-headed. It's a big honour to play such a central character in such a beloved show, and I absolutely love what I do. It's a dream come true for me. It gives me a platform to say who I am and what I think, give it to ya straight from the nag's gob.

I know a lot of people see me as some sort of jack-the-lad, a bit of an airhead. One of the things I hear most often when I meet people is that they're surprised what I'm like in person. So I'd like to give a pipe into who I really am, in my own words.

One thing about me, I am what I am. I'm an East Ender and we're a certain sort. We're a bit coarse, we say what we think, we have our own little walk, like penguins, a bit of a swagger.

One thing, any kids reading this – I ain't no role model. Really, I ain't. I swear, I drink, I do a lot that I shouldn't. I'm a product of the inner city, a broken home, life on the streets. There's nothing in that to look up to, nor down on. It's just as it is. You gotta be your own person, not follow some celebrity.

I'm not trying to tell people what to do, or come over as like, 'I made these mistakes so you don't have to.' I'm just saying how I feel, how life's shaped me and if you take anything from that, great. If ya don't, great too. I think people have to go their own way, I really do.

I think there's something a bit weird about people who arrive fully cooked, completely sorted, get everything right first time. I didn't but I wouldn't have wanted to. They say you ain't a jockey until you've fallen off ten times, and if you're a motor racer who never crashes, you ain't going quick enough. Life's like that. Take my advice, don't take my advice. Fuck things up a bit, life gets interesting that way.

So I don't set out to offend anyone but I ain't gonna paint myself as something I'm not. What you see in the following pages is me, not some toned-down, cleaned-up version. Warts 'n'all. Fucking big warts too in some cases. There's quite a bit of swearing, and a lot of straight talk. A bit of anger and a lot of love.

Nowadays this is a risk. You are only ever one sentence away from a major career-ending shit storm.

I look at someone like Jeremy Clarkson and I wonder if he had some sort of self-destructive impulse. I see something of that in myself. I went through a period in my career where I was pushing the line constantly. I'm not sure I had the intention of screwing everything up but that's how it turned out.

I nearly threw it all away: drink, drugs, doing too many films and not always worrying about the quality. You've got to play the game, adapt very quickly nowadays. The days of Oliver Reed are gone unfortunately.

So I've had an up and down life – and I've tried to write down some of the stuff that I've learned here.

It might surprise some people. Some of it surprised me. I'd never really thought about politics or anything like that before I wrote this book and it was interesting to me to put down what I thought on paper and see my ideas developing. It was interesting to do a bit of research too. Never thought I'd say that. I found out a bit about my manor I never knew before.

Not all of it was easy to put down. Contrary to what people think of me, I'm a bit soft when it comes to thinking about all the love I have in my life, and some of the love I've lost. Did I cry? Of course not, I'm a bloke. I was just suffering from hay fever, that's all.

In this book, I've tried to be as honest as I always do, to give it to you straight. This is my chance to show the real me. That might offend some people, and to them, I respectfully say, 'Stick it up your bottles.'

I also want to thank you, the people who like me and have shown an interest in me over the years – my fans, for want of a better word. I am blessed to be doing the job I've had since the age of fourteen. Acting is a job I love to do. To do it for the last twenty-odd years, all my adult life, and to love it, and to look forward to it, and to feel inspired by it, is a beautiful thing. If people didn't want to watch me I wouldn't have been able to do that. So, thanks. I really mean it.

I

*What do you need in a pub? Beer pumps, a bar, lino,
a dart board and a pool table, maybe a telly for the
football. Chairs and tables, clearly. Maybe a beer
towel for colour. That's it. You're going in to have a
drink and a laugh with your mates – you don't need
a six-course Thai menu and an interior by Laurence
Llewelyn-Bowen to do that.*

I love the East End. It's my home, it made me. I wouldn't
be where I am now if it wasn't for it. The spirit of the
place is in me and I carry it with me wherever I go.

I've grown up with three different East Ends, when
I think about it – the East End my dad and nan would
tell me about, all bomb sites, streams and a life lived
in the street. Then there's the East End I grew up in.
The bomb sites had been replaced by flats, people
stayed indoors a bit more watching TV and stuff –
they never had no tellies in my dad's childhood. Still
there was a bond. You knew your neighbours, looked
out for each other.

Then there's the East End of today. I know it less.
The old rub-a-dubs have gone, the way we talk is

dying out. The area has changed hugely under the influence of outsiders – rich and poor.

I'm not one of those who sit there saying, 'Boo hoo, everything's been wrecked.' London's a town where things change and change fast, always has been. Some things about the new East End are good, for sure. A lot of the old ways of thinking have broken down and that's no bad thing.

My dad reckons that when he was growing up in the early sixties, it was like a paradise. Horses and carts were still on the streets and there was a massive sense of community.

He tells me about New Year's Eve at midnight, when everyone would come out into the street, banging pots and pans, whatever they could get, to welcome in the New Year. All the Blue Star funnels on the ships would sound too. The docks were still busy then and everyone around there worked on them, or at Tate & Lyle up the road.

There was definitely a sense of togetherness then, because so much of life was lived in the street. My dad talks of the streets full of hundreds of men going to work, coming home, off to the football, the pub, the dogs and the speedway.

There was no staying in with the Xbox when he was a kid. West Ham held dog meetings twice a week, stock cars once and speedway once. Speedway was nearly as big as football back then.

As a kid my dad would offer to mind cars, then nick into the dog meet, have a penny on the dogs and be out in time to get his tip from the drivers. When the speedway was on, the place was rammed and there was none of this marshalling or whatever. The kids used to raid the pits to get the riders' goggles.

Even to me it sounds like a different world.

One of the favourite games when he was a kid was getting an old basket on a couple of ropes and trawling it along a ditch. A ditch with animals in it, in the East End!

They'd get sticklebacks and newts out, take them home and put 'em in the bath. I can't imagine a ditch like that in Custom House nowadays. He built rafts to go down the river, played in bomb shelters. The city was still a wreck, so much debris from World War II, that there was always something to find or to do. Dad brought a duckling back with him off the Thames and had it swimming about in the tin bath. Then he fed it a stickleback and it died – he buried it under the tree in the garden.

Some of the stuff they got up to would get you nicked now – building massive bonfires for Guy Fawkes Night on waste ground. One year a rival gang burned their bonfire early so my dad and his mates rebuilt it out of tyres and smoked out the neighbourhood for a week.

What comes over to me from his stories is how much life was lived in the street, how everyone knew everyone. There was fuck all indoors, really, the pubs were always rammed. West Ham, according to my dad, held more than Wembley. I can't quite believe that but if he says it's true, I'm not gonna argue.

When I was growing up, we still had that – little gangs of us roaming about all day – but by then the sticklebacks had gone and we spent our time collecting spliffs rather than birds' eggs. Still, we had a sense of community and most of my childhood was spent roaming about the place, through concrete estates rather than bomb sites.

We had our own entertainment in lots of ways – tagging, breaking into the train yard to spray 'em all up, running around on building sites, diving out of the way of other gangs. It was no worse than my dad's generation got up to really. They had their little mobs who'd fight each other, do a bit of nicking.

Not that my dad did the nicking. He's always been a grafter – went to work in a butcher's shop aged ten for a quid a day. But, as he says, they had nothing, really, so if you wanted much of a better life then there were only a few ways of getting it – villainy chief among them.

That old East End has gone, really. It's not just our street life that has disappeared. It's happened all over the country. Now we're all indoors on our computers or stuck by the TV. Pubs are half empty a lot of the time.

Like all sorts of change, there are some good sides to that and some bad.

Let's start with the good, because too often when people look at the present, they start whining on about how much better it used to be years ago.

Let's be fair, people of my dad's and granddad's generation were pretty intolerant. Some people won't see that as a bad thing, but I do. When you get out and see the world a bit you realize you can't start saying that one group of people is a certain way and basically a bunch of slags and everything that people like you do is fine.

When you get outside the area, you realize there are plenty of people who don't like Cockneys, incredible as that sounds. No, bear with me, it's true. They have their own views of us, some right, some wrong. To some people we're a bunch of criminal wide boys who'd rob their own grannies. That's not right. I have never met anyone who would rob his own granny – one or two junkie scummers aside.

I have known Cockney diamonds and other total wankers. You can't generalize.

But there's no doubt that in my dad's day people had narrower views of the world than they do now.

Homophobia and racism are the modern terms, though if you'd mentioned homophobia to my dad he'd have thought it was an album by The Who.

From the outside my dad might have looked homophobic but I don't think it ever crossed his mind there was a problem with that. He was a bloke, of course he didn't like gay men, poofs, as he would have called them. There was one sort of man who tolerated gay men and that was another gay man.

And you have to remember, when they were growing up being gay was illegal. So even the government was saying that being gay was wrong, and you can't blame a bunch of basically quite uneducated people in the East End for agreeing with them, particularly when gay people kept their heads down at the time so you weren't aware of knowing them in the way you might today.

A similar thing with racism, really. Our area – Custom House – was very white at that time. If a black fella walked in a pub everyone would turn their heads, it was unheard of. Black and Asian people were more around Hackney and a bit further in.

So the older generation never had any dealings with anyone but white people, and other Cockneys at that. Yes, they were racist but I prefer to think of them as a bit closed in and narrow-minded rather than bad. They were good people but just hadn't been exposed to much of the world.

Of course, the reality of those things is a bit more and a bit less complicated than it might look from the outside. For a start, you didn't need to be gay to suffer from homophobia and just because you were gay didn't mean that you would.

My mum had a close friend who was very flamboyant, very obviously gay. Strangely, he was quite accepted in my area. It was like, 'He might be a poof, but he's our poof.' The fact is, if people have long enough to get used to people – and he had grown up around there – their prejudices tend to vanish.

This is peculiar – it's like they were saying, 'The gay man I know is OK, it's the ones I have never met I hate, despite knowing fuck all about them.'

He got his share of homophobia, I'm sure, but all the really bad things that happened to him happened outside the area, or so he told my mum.

I actually suffered from homophobia, despite not being gay. To my mates, and some who weren't quite as matey, being an actor is exactly the same as being homosexual. There is no difference between the two. The bullying I got was sometimes horrible. I got 'actress' and 'poofter' and all the rest of it. It got so bad that I stopped telling people anything I was doing and used to sneak off to the acting and slide on back over the maisonettes smoking weed before anyone could even tell. It was like living two lives.

I'm not saying it made my life hell, just difficult. It got boring more than anything but I did get a glimpse into what it must be like to have someone sticking them labels on you every day and wanting to drag you down because of it.

Things have changed nowadays of course. There was an influx of black and Asian people into the area, and then, after City Airport, ExCel and the Olympics, house prices started going through the roof.

A maisonette near my mother-in-law's went for 300 grand the other day. It's a two-bedroomed, tiny little place. But people want to live there because of how close it is to the City.

Some of this influence has been good. People are more mixed in than they were, a lot more tolerant. However, the place seems to have lost something to me. There's a bit of an angry edge to it. Why is that? I'm sure there would be some who'd say, 'It's a bunch of foreigners coming in.' To me it's not that straightforward.

The East End is a dock area, so there's always been a mix of people. It was known as a Jewish area years ago and all sorts have always settled there.

We've had some really brilliant people come into the area who have done nothing but add to it. One of them who settled on the manor was Squadron Leader Mahindra Singh Pujji – a Battle of Britain hero with balls bigger than King Kong. He fought non-stop through the Battle of Britain, then did fighter sweeps over Europe, conducting low-level attacks. After that he went to the Western Desert and after that to Burma to fight the Japanese. There he won the Distinguished Flying Cross. They reported it in the *London Gazette*:

> This officer has flown on many reconnaissance sorties over Japanese occupied territory, often in adverse monsoon weather. He has obtained much valuable information of enemy troop movements and dispositions, which enabled an air offensive to be maintained against the Japanese troops throughout the monsoon. Flight Lieutenant Pujji has shown himself to be a skilful and determined pilot who has always displayed outstanding leadership and courage.

According to UKIP and other melts, we should have told him to fuck off back to India.

John Charles was born here – the first black player to represent England; Lennox Lewis just down the road in Stratford to Jamaican parents. Linda Lewis was an actress and singer who came from Custom House. First- and second-generation immigrants have added a lot to the area. Idris Elba, who I'm right proud of, was born in Canning Town to African parents. I knew him before he had his big break with *The Wire*, brilliant TV, when he was struggling a bit. It's terrific he's gone over to Hollywood and smashed it. A local boy and a proper actor.

Let's not pretend it was all roses, though. Immigration was met with some resistance and you can see why. No one likes change and everyone thinks the way they grew up with things is the way it always was. People who didn't like immigration were seen as bigots or evil but a lot of it was just the natural reaction to seeing any sort of change. It's not that different to how people in small communities all over the world feel about outsiders coming in in numbers.

So then you get a sort of vicious circle happening. People feel mugged off by the immigrants, the immigrants feel mugged off by the people who are already there and before you know it, it's gone a bit tits up.

You've got an immigrant group coming into an area where they're not always welcome. The whole place is a shit heap when it comes to opportunity and they are on the bottom of that shit heap. So no wonder some of the kids turn a bit lairy. You're despised by those around you and have no real chance of getting out of the place. That's going to make anyone get fucked off.

On top of that you've got a whole other load of people coming in and buying up the houses. These people have got a lot of money and are living a life you can only dream about. Which is likely to get you even more fucked off. Us and them, all that.

Then all the people who have been there for years cash in and move out to Essex and suddenly there's no community any more. No one knows each other like they did.

That said, London has always had immigrants, it's an immigrant city, and on the whole people have got on very well. The East End itself has always been right at the front of that – having the docks in it. Some of the friction is just that – people rubbing against each other while things settle down. Some of it's nothing at all to do with immigration and just down to poverty and lack of opportunity. It will be interesting to see how the East End looks in thirty years' time.

To the average person in the street I may appear like a foul-mouthed Cockney who's just crawled out of the gutter but, compared to the people I grew up with, I have the polish of The Duchess of Kent.

I won't be there, but that's nothing to do with immigration, or rather it is – the immigration of money.

One of the things that has changed around Custom House since I was a nipper is that the old boozers have been flattened and yuppie flats put up – that disgusts me. Pretty much, when the boozers went from the East End, so did I.

They were hubs for the community just like The Vic in *EastEnders*. All the kids knew they'd find their dad in one of them if he wasn't indoors. They were magical places. In Prince Regent Lane there were three boozers all in one strip, old boozers like King Henry VIII might have drunk in – you had the Prince of Wales, the Nottingham Arms and The Barge.

That smell of the pub was wonderful to me as a boy. In them days you could smoke in the pub and you had that stale tobacco, the beer in the air, there would be no music necessarily, just that hum of Cockney voices, a big echo of laughter and then it would go quiet before bursting out loud again. There was a music to it, almost a rhythm.

Some of the East End pubs were listed buildings, and they burnt to the ground. Two weeks later, they've whacked flats up. I find it depressing.

People don't seem to go to the pub like they did any more. I don't know what's changed. Supermarkets offering cheap drink? The smoking ban was never going to help.

And gastropubs. What are they about? I don't come into a pub to have a Small Batch coffee and tuna drizzled in jus, whatever that is. I come in for a pint of beer, a game of pool and a packet of pork scratchings.

Maybe even a jellied eel, for those of you who want to take the piss.

My idea of hell is eternity in a poncy wine bar. How anyone ever drinks somewhere like that, I don't know. There's no atmosphere, no dodgy characters everyone knows bowling in, no kids sitting smoking on the steps outside. Who wants to sit in a pub full of blokes in suits? It's meant to have 'ambience'. Well let me tell you, a pub full of pissed-up Cockneys smoking their heads off while they take the piss out of each other and everything around them has plenty of ambience.

I don't condone underage drinking or smoking at all, but when I was a kid the pub actually kept us out of trouble. We'd sit on the steps and hope to nip in when no one was looking to finish up the pints – mine-sweeping we called it.

What do you need in a pub? Beer pumps, a bar, lino, a dart board and a pool table, maybe a telly for the football. Chairs and tables, clearly. Maybe a beer towel for colour. That's it. You're going in to have a drink and a laugh with your mates – you don't need a six-course Thai menu and an interior by Laurence Llewelyn-Bowen to do that. It cheats the customer.

I cannot stand the idea of restaurant food in pubs.

I mean, what would happen if you decided you were going to take the other half out for a nice Thai meal and when you got into the restaurant there was a bunch of fat bastards in sportswear drinking cheap lager, filling out betting slips and talking bollocks in a loud voice? You'd feel short changed, particularly when they told you they didn't do Thai food at all and all you were getting was a pickled egg. That's the equivalent of what happens to me when I end up in a gastropub.

It's not just pubs that are under threat, of course.

Whole communities face eviction in some cases from developers. Drugs explode because people can't see any other way of making a living and before you know it you're in a scary area.

The pubs were the old East End for me. I miss hanging around on the steps of a rough old boozer waiting for your old man to give you a quid for chips. The one my dad drank in had sawdust on the floor to mop up the beer and, to be honest, the blood that was spilled there.

I'm not going to pretend it was a paradise where we all went around hugging each other in a state of bliss. Tear-ups were regular as. I remember seeing numerous tear-ups outside the Nottingham Arms – geezers who'd been on the piss all day punching the granny out of each other. We'd stand over the road by the chip shop watching it spill out into the road. Then it would all get sorted out and they'd go back in the boozer. You'd get these fellas coming in who had something about them – very well-known men, boats, dangerous men. That gave the place an edge.

As a kid you looked up to them. Yes, you had to learn to hold your hands up or people would walk all over you but I don't think that's a bad thing.

A working-class upbringing is not all glamour, however, as I am about to show.

Some of the stuff that went on in them places would be enough to scar you for life. I would warn anyone of a nervous disposition to possibly look away now until the end of the chapter. This is life in all its glory and strangeness I'm about to tell you here and I think it might be a little bit much for some people. If you saw this in a film you might think it had come out of the imagination of a twisted degenerate who wanted locking up for the public good, but it happened right in front of my eyes.

I am going to describe what might be seen as my first sexual experience, which went on in one of them boozers, my mind has blanked which one, when I was about ten. Look, ya've been warned. This is not for the faint-hearted. Nor the weak-stomached. Nor quite a lot of other people, actually. To be honest, I wish I could blank it from my mind. So, that said, here goes.

It was one geezer's birthday in the pub and at about noon they got a couple of strippers in. I think all people are beautiful in their own way, I've got no time for this idea that there's only one standard for the way people should look. However, these women could best be described as rough and ready. They was ready and they was certainly rough – a bit of the Stone Age figure thing going on, never see twenty-one again, nor forty-one either, you get the picture? This isn't some sweeping judgement on people of a certain age, either. We are judged by our actions, not how we look, and by their actions they was filth.

Anyway there's fifty or so geezers in there and they start the act, trying to get someone from the audience involved in it. One of my mates, who I won't name, was about sixteen at the time. The East End breeds some funny characters and he was as funny as they get. He gets up on stage with them and, in front of fifty geezers – make sure ya ready, not just eaten or nothing like that – she puts on a strap-on dildo and does him up the bottle. He was really into it. In the middle of the day in front of a crowd of Cockneys goading them on. Try doin' the Lambeth Walk after that, you slag. I was not party to the goading. Not at all. It frightened the life out of me and I had a hard time understanding quite what was going on. I can still see the expression on his face. It was bizarrely refined, like Sherlock Holmes enjoying a bit of violin.

I had that buzzing around in me nut for the rest of the day, couldn't get it out of me nut, really. He had a fixation about the old Khyber. When we went out and had a few drinks, he'd whip out a funnel, or a pipe. One of my clearest early memories is of him stood on his head with his legs wide open and a funnel sticking out of his arse, having vodka poured into it. He said it got him drunk quicker, went to his brain faster. I can't work that out – your mouth's nearer your brain ain't it? I'm not a doctor and neither was he, although I never found out what happened to him later in life. Perhaps he went down the medical route. Or hospitality – he used to experiment with various drinks. One time he poured Bloody Mary in there. He fainted, I don't know why. Well, I do know why, he'd been filled up with vodka and tomato juice. He wandered off. We found him by following the trail of tomato juice.

This is why, when people find me a little bit direct, a little bit rude, they have to understand where I'm coming from. To the average person in the street I may appear like a foul-mouthed Cockney who's just crawled out of the gutter but, compared to the people I grew up with, I have the polish of The Duchess of Kent. Really, I'm shy. My fiancée Joanne says I'm shy anyway, but I suppose that anyone's shy compared to a bloke who's prepared to do a headstand while people use his arse as a cocktail mixer.

I wonder where he is now? Probably doing a headstand somewhere. I wish him all the best, though, he was a lovely geezer, if a bit odd.

There were other characters – like a mad homeless bloke called Ken. We used to give him little bits of our drinks, maybe the odd snout, coins, that sort of thing. Some of the older boys, though, used to be a bit cruel to him. One day they spiked his drink with LSD and chained him to a lamppost. I felt very sorry for him, out there in the sun, unable to get away, red hot tripping off his nut. They released him later in the day, came along and chucked him in the back of a van. It was a great advert for not taking drugs, chained up there on the main road.

He was all right, I saw him a few days later but there was no need for what they did to him and it upset me. Nowadays I would probably have called the Fire Brigade to come and get him out but in them days the idea would never have entered my head. It was depressing. People used to give him a clump the whole time, though some were kind to him. How do you get there, to have no one at all, and be at the mercy of any twisted slag who wants to take it out on ya? I don't know but I know it made a lasting impression on me seeing someone that vulnerable and defenceless. People shouldn't end up like that, we shouldn't let 'em.

So, to be fair, it's difficult to argue that the place has allowed standards to slip.

There wasn't the gang thing when we was growing up, though – we was one area, one force. If another manor came over to our manor – Limehouse or Hackney, maybe somewhere south of the water – we'd all stick together and have it. Now they're stabbing each other if you live in a different street.

Still, if it hadn't have been for the kids, I'd have probably stayed there. Even until just a few years ago we lived in Joanne's little flat in Custom House. It wasn't easy there after I got famous, our house was like Stonehenge, we got so many people gawping at it. It was like the eighth wonder of the world. Even our bin was nicked. Have you tried getting a new bin? You'd have a better chance asking the council for a Jacuzzi. It took weeks and there I was prowling about the neighbourhood with bags of rubbish trying to sneak 'em into the neighbours' bins. I don't know what I would have said if I'd got snapped doing it. 'Dyer hits new low bin-dipping,' probably.

I didn't mind living there because I was still happy – even though we ended up with a TV that was almost bigger than one wall. We lived there until about 2009, never thought to move really.

What changed it for me was realizing my daughter was starting to talk like the kids in the gangs do, kissing her teeth, all that. That wouldn't have bothered me so much but I could see it wouldn't be long before she got exposed to a very savage and unforgiving world. I felt like I was losing her to a whole new culture that I didn't understand. I had to get her out of there, lively.

It sounds sexist – and probably is – but it would have bothered me less if she'd been a boy. I think you naturally feel more protective towards your daughters while, to an extent, you have to let your sons fight their own battles.

She was also getting a right attitude on her and I feared she might go off the rails.

Then – it was a bit like the straw that broke the camel's back – Joanne was in the flat on her own and this hand just comes through the window and tries to nick her bag. I didn't feel safe leaving her or my daughter there any more.

So we did what a lot of people did and fucked off to Essex. Overnight it was like I was a stranger in my own area. I thought, 'I don't know anyone round here any more, I don't understand the mentality.'

Do I miss it? Of course, it's my home and it's left its mark on me. It's still a great place but it was just my time to go.

2

If I learned one thing off my mum, it's that all the money in the world won't help you unless you can get up in the morning, look in the mirror and be satisfied that you're not one of life's slags.

Women have been the most important people in my life, by far. My dad got booted out when I was nine and he wasn't exactly a new man when it came to childcare before that.

Don't get me wrong, I love my dad, but it was my mum and my nan who brought me up.

The women in my life have all been true East Enders – you could almost cast some of them directly in the soap. Take my nan – five foot nothing, smokes like a chimney, or did until the doctor gave her the red card on that, swears like a trooper and could knock a charging bull over with a headbutt. She is a tough woman who is never afraid to stand up for herself.

My mum is a huge influence on me, massive. She's the kindest person I know and a pacifist. She works teaching prison inmates to read and write. She's someone who can be massively proud of themselves because they've given to the world, not taken from it.

If I learned one thing off my mum, it's that all the money in the world won't help you unless you can get up in the morning, look in the mirror and be satisfied that you're not one of life's slags.

People often ask me about my ideal woman. Well, I've got it, ain't I, in Joanne? Had it since I was fourteen. Fire, personality, a bit of spirit. A lot of spirit in Joanne's case. Too much spirit, sometimes.

I've been with Joanne for nearly my whole life – she's my fiancée and may even be my wife by the time this is published, if she finally decides when and where she wants the wedding. We've been together for twenty-five years, since we met at school. We bonded through the drama class. It was the only lesson I was any good at – she was good at everything, teachers' pet, on first name terms with some of them.

I think she started to look at me a bit differently when she saw I could act. I certainly looked at her – she was always the best in dance class.

It's funny how life throws up these little coincidences – we had to do our drama exam together. I can't honestly remember what it was about but I like to think it was some sort of love scene. Maybe it was me and her having a go at each other, that would have been good preparation too.

I remember she got an A and I got a B, and that fucked me off. I'm over it now, mainly.

Joanne is my whole world – that can be for good reasons and for bad reasons. She's a real force. I've taken her on this journey and she's struggled with it as I have. Of course it was the path that I chose and she sort of rolled into it. I sometimes feel guilty about that and I know I would not have a career without her support.

She lives with me, she listens to me snoring, she washes my dirty pants. So to see me getting this amazing recognition, and to see me put on a pedestal, she literally cannot believe it. She cannot get her head round it.

She's the love of my life, there's no two ways about it. I think of her every day and when she's not there I miss her with an ache in my heart. We're so close, it's stupid. The idea of being parted from her fills me with dread, far worse than dying or illness or anything. I know we will get old – if we're lucky – and one of us will have to spend time without the other one. I hope it's me who goes first. In that way, she makes me a coward.

There have been times in the past when we've both come to an agreement and thought maybe it's run its course. It's true that we sometimes detest each other and challenge each other. But something always brings us back.

I'm immensely proud of her. People go on about the rights and wrongs of women looking after the kids or working from home. She's done both. When I was 'resting' – i.e. unemployed – she was working. Now I'm working, she's a mother to three kids of vastly different ages.

It is difficult to keep relationships on track, especially with the kids thing but I honestly couldn't imagine being with anyone else.

We've been through everything together and I couldn't have got to where I am without her. I was the flighty one, doing all the mad stuff, while she held the family together, made sure the kids got to school and were washed, fed and clothed.

She's an incredible mother too. She can have a heart to heart with Dani, turn out Sunnie for school like she's ready to pass a military inspection and – unbelievably – get Arty to do as he's told. That alone makes her a magician, as far as I'm concerned. I can't do nothing with him, he does what he wants around me. I only have to turn my back and there's cornflakes hitting the ceiling when I'm looking after him.

We are a team. I'm like Paul Gascoigne, she's like David Batty. I mean it as a compliment comparing Joanne to a hard-as-nails Yorkshire midfielder, famous for murderous tackles. Obviously she doesn't look like David Batty, who has the kind of face that wouldn't do him any favours in front of a jury.

It's not a perfect comparison. For a start, she's from East London, not Yorkshire. But she's not above giving me what is known in football terms as a 'reducer'. Some actors, apparently, have difficulty keeping grounded. They've always got people blowing smoke up their arses. No fear of that for me. If I ever get above myself, she will come in with a sliding tackle from the halfway line to knock me back down to earth. In fact, she's not above continuing it in the tunnel after the game either, or trying to get me in the car park.

I think that's a good thing.

I can't argue with her anyway. She's ten times brighter than me, ten times faster in a tear-up. I'm like the tricky winger who hasn't got quite enough in his locker to avoid the left back putting him into row Z.

Most of the time we work together. She takes care of the day-to-day stuff and it's a good job she does because I would not have a clue.

You need the Battys of this world so the Gascoignes can get the room to play. She wins the ball, so to speak, and lays it off to me to score.

Me and Joanne are a team. I'm like Paul Gascoigne, she's like David Batty.

Me and Joanne have had our ups and downs, and even broken up for a spell. That was the worst time of my life. I was utterly and completely lost, doing mad, self-destructive things that seemed like fun at the time but, looking back, were just covering up how unhappy I was.

Did we meet too young? Neither of us had any time to experience life without each other, so maybe that caused our break-up, simple curiosity. We met before we were halfway through our teens.

The person you are when you are fourteen is not the same person you are when you're twenty or thirty and the person you are when you're thirty isn't the person you are when you're forty. So it's remarkable that, in all that time, as we've changed so much, we still love each other.

When she met me I was just a Herbert running around the East End, no education, no thoughts in my head beyond a bottle of Lambrini and the next spliff. At thirty-eight, we've had so many experiences together it's mad. I've been directed by literary giants, sat down to dinner with them. I've met people from so far outside my background they may as well be from Mars. She's gone through motherhood, all the insecurity of being with an actor, watched me get famous.

And yet still, after all that, well, I may as well not even go on writing here. There are no words to say how I feel about her.

We're so close it's almost like we're the same person. She feels like half of me – literally my better half. It's not that I'm unhappy without her, it's that I'm not me. I'm something less, something that doesn't quite work.

Don't get me wrong, we're not always lovey dovey, stars in our eyes over each other. She challenges me every day of my life. Every minute of my life, it feels like sometimes. She is not afraid to give it me in the earhole if I step out of line, which I often do.

I try to please her and don't always succeed, but it feels good to do little things for her. She's a big fan of José Mourinho and whenever I see him on the telly I'll tape him for her. I know she doesn't like putting her hand in the cold water in the sink if it's covering dishes so I'll always do that for her. If we've rowed, then sometimes I won't. I'll leave it for a bit and then feel stupid and guilty and go and do it. Every day of my life I try to be a better person. Most days, I don't manage it. Some more than others.

She'll test my behaviour. If she thinks I'm changing, she'll let me know. There's a Danny Dyer she knows and the one she sees on the street and sometimes she doesn't like the one she sees on the street because she knows I'm just playing up to my image. She won't have that.

She challenges me on my laziness all the time around the house. I still can't turn a washing machine on. Arty can, I can't. She will challenge me on that every day and yet I still can't be arsed with it. I go out and I graft me bollocks off, so it's hard to fight the urge to come home and lay on the settee after a twelve-hour day.

However, there has to be give-and-take. I'll take the bin out. I don't normally do it, but if I remember things like that it makes her happy.

She's made me iron shirts before, out of spite. I fucked them up deliberately. I don't know how you fuck up ironing a shirt but I did. It's just not my forté. And if I did do everything what would she do? I work to earn the money, if I came back home and did all the washing, ironing and cleaning, where does she come into it? It's meant to be a team effort. I'm only having a laugh, don't worry.

The stress of having to pay bills – I never put that on her. I earn the readies, that's nothing she'll ever have to worry about. And I respect what she does. I come home sometimes and the pile of ironing is bigger than her, it's like *Close Encounters of the Third Kind*.

At the end of the day, though, none of these little domestics matter. I know she loves me with all her heart and I love her with all mine too.

I probably shouldn't say this, but I've done jobs where I've had my lines written for me by the best writers in the world, and I sometimes do use those, particularly if I've had a row with the missus, in a wooing-back kind of way.

When you've got kids, your relationship revolves around the children so you start thinking, 'When was the last time we actually tongued each other, you know, a full-on tongue?'

Sometimes I can be quite distant from my missus, maybe we haven't been physical in a while, and I'll say stuff like, 'Your potential kiss has got my mind and body aching.' Now that's a line from the song 'Unfinished Sympathy' by Massive Attack. It's a beautiful little line, and I don't think there's anything wrong with using it because I've heard it and it makes me think of Jo. All right, you might think it's a bit naughty because I'm making out it's come from my nut. But it has a truth about it. I think it might be a bit obvious if I try to track a bit of Harold Pinter in – the Nobel Prize-winning playwright who was such a big influence on me. It's another level if I come out with:

> The lamps are golden.
> Afternoon leans, silently.
> She dances in my life.
> The white day burns.

I reckon she would suss me. I don't think she's gonna be suffering that too much. I try, though, that's what I'm trying to say.

Am I a new man? Well, compared to my dad's generation, I'm metrosexual number one. I might not do the graft with the kids – I freely admit that – but I'm always there to take them places, always there to stick a bit of Lego together.

3

Media training wasn't for me. They said they could do a lot to polish my image but in the end I told them to fuck themselves.

When you're in the public eye there are people who will offer to represent you to the press and to train you to deal with them.

About ten years ago, I met a bloke who said he'd train me not to say anything controversial in the press, not to court notoriety, so to speak. I told him to fuck himself. The thing is, I don't want to live in a world where people are afraid to speak their minds. I tell you what, I wish I'd had the guys at *EastEnders* around back then. They don't tell me what to say, just give me advice on how the press works and how to deal with being in the spotlight. That's what media training should be about.

Bad media training is what's wrong with a lot of our politicians, among other things. They all look like they're off *Thunderbirds*, plastic faces, reading from the same script. People don't trust 'em because they don't say what they mean. I wonder if half of 'em even know what they mean any more, they're just these insipid little twats afraid of causing offence to anyone. They wear the same clobber, have the same barnets, you can't tell one from another.

It's also what's wrong with bands nowadays. Look at One Direction – to me their music isn't bad but there's no soul to it. I do not understand how they've sold more than The Beatles and The Stones. How can that be? I've met 'em and they're OK but pretty unremarkable kinds of blokes. Most of 'em are so bland and nothingy that you wonder if they could get an automatic door to open for 'em.

Do we want unremarkable blokes as our pop stars? Surely you'd rather have Prince or some nutter like Björk than the latest nobody on autotune.

I've seen holograms with more presence.

They've had media training, along with all the others that come off *The X Factor*. Who would you rather listen to in an interview, Harry Styles or Noel Gallagher? I'm sure Noel would have been advised against calling his brother a slag but it's a sight more entertaining than Harry telling you what his favourite colour is.

Years ago pop stars – even for young kids – used to have a bit about them. You look at the old Slade with

Noddy Holder. If he'd had media training it would have been 'Drop the mirrors on your titfer, son, get your barnet cut and shave the strange 'n' weird. And stop talking in that Brummie voice, no one understands a word you're saying.' Yet he's got more talent in his little finger than most of the Top 40 put together. Do an experiment. Stick on 'Cum On Feel The Noize' and then put some simpering ballads by One Direction on afterwards. Halfway through you'll bin the 1D and go back and listen to Slade again.

Do we want unremarkable blokes as our pop stars? Surely you'd rather have Prince or some nutter like Björk than the latest nobody on autotune.

I just don't think that people are so narrow-minded to reject people who don't look exactly like you expect them to, sound exactly like you expect them to and talk exactly like you expect them to. You look at the charts years ago, they were full of amazing bands from all sorts of backgrounds.

I like a bit of the old soul. Can you imagine soul legend Gil Scott-Heron meeting the media training crew off *X Factor*. 'Well, Gil, what are you planning to talk about in your interview for *We Love Pop*?' 'Revolution and racial prejudice.' They'd drop a bollock. I'll tell you this, though, you listen to a record by any of those old soul singers – Aretha Franklin, James Brown, Curtis Mayfield, and you know you've had an experience. Sexualness in your earholes. All the manufactured pop nowadays is by people who've seen nothing, thought about nothing and done nothing, and that's exactly how it sounds.

In fact, four out of five members in most bands seem to be there just to look pretty. Is that a job? I mean, when they ask you what you do, what do you say? 'I sit on a stool pretending to lip sync.' Cos that's what it is. People in some of these bands don't even sing on the original records. They are pretending that they're faking it. They're basically less use to the band than their own roadies. Seriously. If the bloke who drives the tour bus goes missing, they're fucked. If three of the band fall off a cliff, the show can go on without a hitch. I couldn't hold my head up in public.

The modern day is all about manipulating your image, controlling how people see you. I've given up on it. It's impossible, I think. I'd rather call things as I see 'em and take the consequences than try to be something I'm not.

The funny thing is, some of the people who are setting people up like this are far worse themselves. Take Max Clifford.

Max Clifford, to me, was everything that was wrong with the British press. I never liked him from the start – something weird about him.

4

If you're looking for happy endings, try Walt Disney.
This is football. It's meant to break your heart.

West Ham is a proper football club. It's right in the
middle of the community, you have to go through
streets of terraced houses to get there – this ain't some
soulless new stadium with plenty of parking and a
nice fat A road running up to the door. It feels well
urban, tower blocks and houses crowding in against
the ground. The roads around it are dirty, full of
traffic.

If Chelsea or Tottenham, and especially Millwall are
visiting you'll find a real buzz in the air – the streets
thick with riot police, the smell of horses, and the hot
dogs that it's rumoured some of the horses may one
day become, mingling in with the fumes of the street,
Cockney voices everywhere. This is London, no
mistake.

You see the old London too, great rolling fat blokes
in the pie and mash shops tucking into steaming plate-
fuls, the wide boys and the chancers. Some bloke built
like a Hereford bull, wearing his West Ham shirt and

singing his heart out. And of course the hard men are there too – the boats, them who seem to have a little aura about 'em. It's intimidating for other teams – you know if you've come to have it here you will get it, because we've got plenty.

That said, it's a family club too. I'd have no qualms about taking my kids there. You know the hooligans ain't looking for them anyway.

West Ham fans are proper fans. Yes, we have hooligans and are even famous for them, but there's a brilliant sense of humour at the ground. You saw that with the YouTube thing when some Chelsea estate agents pretending to be hard men chucked that bloke off the tube in Paris. To make mugs of Chelsea, showing them up for what they are, West Ham released a video of fans helping a black bloke onto the tube.

We don't get the plastic fans that some of the bigger clubs do – glory hunters. You might say that's because we haven't had much glory and that's sort of fair comment. The words of the club song 'I'm Forever Blowing Bubbles' say 'Fortune's always hiding' and that's about right. But this is an authentic East End club. There's no competition around here, apart from Leyton Orient, the smaller team, who for some reason hate us – both their fans. I always root for them but they hate us.

Of course, we're in it for the winning but winning means more to us than it does to clubs like Man

United. They take winning for granted. You could see the looks on their faces when they were losing the other season. They looked like a flying saucer had just landed in the middle of the pitch. It was beyond their understanding.

The fans honestly didn't know how to cope with it. It was as if some of them were saying, 'This isn't what I paid my money for, to watch a game where I don't know the outcome. I come here for certain victory because I can't get a sense of self-worth any other way.' When they lost three games in a row it was like it was the end of the world.

Of course, not all their fans are like that and some have been with them through thick and thin, since they were in the old Division 2 and even before. It must get right on the tits of all them who've been there for the two decades or so between league titles to be surrounded by all these new fans who don't understand that football is basically about thwarted ambition, bitter disappointment, disgust and resentment all made amazing by flashing moments of brilliance. They don't know that football is like life, everything passes apart from Crystal Palace.

The certainty for most of us when our club is being successful is that failure is just around the corner. Those who don't remember that are likely to turn bitter.

It would mug me right off to follow a team that always won. I know from working in acting that one of the things that keeps people's arses glued to the seats is suspense. You go and watch a James Bond film and you've no idea how Bond is going to get off the table with the laser beam aimed at his bollocks and beat the bad guys. That's interesting enough but watching West Ham you have no idea if the hero actually will get out or if his nuts will be fried which, in this case means the championship and away trips to Rotherham. Personally, I'd go for the laser beam.

You have no idea when the next high is coming. It could be in a few minutes, it could be seasons away.

So you can't be watching sides like West Ham if you're of a nervous disposition or if you haven't got any character. Maybe this is why people end up supporting big teams miles away from where they live – they basically haven't got the bollocks to stick with their local side – no backbone. They make the mistake of assuming football is about entertainment. It's not. It's one big mirror to your life – years of boredom punctuated by grief, anger and occasional bliss.

West Ham don't expect to win every game and when we do win unexpectedly, it comes as a real treat. Still the best game of football I've seen was the West Ham–Liverpool FA Cup final in 2006. We lost that but I have never known any emotions like it.

I know Jamie Redknapp and he'd got me tickets – unfortunately for the Liverpool end. I didn't care, I was celebrating like a madman when we scored and, obviously, taking a bucket of shit from the Scousers. We scored twice, they equalized, we went ahead again and they nicked it in the last minute, going on to win on penalties. Steven Gerrard. Too good on the day.

I had lost about four stone in sweat by the end of it. You don't get that if you're looking for your tenth FA cup or twenty-first league victory. That's the beauty of being a West Ham fan.

There is a certain kind of fan who follows the big teams just because they're winners. What is that about? Is your sense of self-worth so low that you can't bear to be associated ever with failure? Have you no bollocks? If you're looking for

We've never won the top flight, though we've come close. We did win the World Cup for England, but that's another story.

happy endings, try Walt Disney. This is football. It's meant to break your heart.

How do you hold your head up in public if you're one of these Cockney Reds, supporting Man U or Liverpool? There is nothing worse than some jumped-up prick from Colchester going on about Manchester United, 'our' history, all that. If you're from Colchester support Colchester. These people say, 'Well I've supported Manchester United since I was a kid.' Why?

Because they were a better team than Colchester. It disgusts me. You do not choose your football team, it chooses you.

If you support Raith Rovers and you go to their little ground, and it only holds four or five thousand people, it don't matter. You're part of the buzz up there. You know that Rangers are going to come to your town and try to nick three points. Most of the time they will, but on the odd occasion you're going to beat them and you're going to walk out of there on cloud nine. You're gonna buzz and float all the way home, just because you nicked three points off a big club.

I once saw two Cockneys in a pub, one in a Man U shirt, the other in a Liverpool shirt, arguing with each other: 'We won this, we won that.' Who's we? I thought, 'You pair of slags. I bet you don't know one Man United song, or you shouldn't because all their songs are about being Northerners or coalminers or whatever they do.' These people don't know anything about the soul of football. They shouldn't be allowed to get involved in football. It's embarrassing. If we all supported who we wanted to, everyone would go for Barcelona.

Your team is in your blood, an expression of who you are, your local identity. This is why West Ham fans are the best in the world. That's a fact, proven by science. They've done tests on it, I'm sure, but they're too afraid to release the results because they're afraid all the big teams will get the hump.

Look at it this way: it's easy to support someone who's always winning. The test comes in the tough times and West Ham have had more than most. We don't suddenly desert our team because of years of failure, including having the best squad ever to get relegated. We've never won the top flight, though we've come close. We did win the World Cup for England, but that's another story. We were a force during the eighties, the McAvennie and Cottee years. I cherish those years, when we was powerful and we had the powerful support to back it.

But I fear for West Ham, I really do. We're moving out of the Boleyn Ground – Upton Park – and into the Olympic Stadium. I remember when we had the Chicken Run down the side of the pitch, the fans close enough almost to touch the players. Will that be the case in the new stadium? I doubt it.

I don't know what they're going to do with the old stadium, if they're going to knock it down or build flats on it. I know there are a lot of Gooners out there who can't go nowhere near Highbury, nostalgia kills them. It must be a horrible feeling. I can't imagine what it's going to be like. Upton Park is beautiful, just the feel of it in the middle of that council estate. It's all going to be gone.

Now we're going to have a running track between us and the pitch? And really, the stadium ain't even in West Ham. It's quite Essexy. I'm scared it'll change the

5

I know what it's like for kids nowadays who grow up in one-parent families and how easy it is to go off the rails. It's not that you need someone clipping you round the King Lear 24/7, it's more having someone to model your behaviour on.

My dad is a great bloke but he wasn't around all that much. He left when I was nine so it was my mum and my nan who brought me up.

I know what it's like for kids nowadays who grow up in one-parent families and how easy it is to go off the rails. It's not that you need someone clipping you round the King Lear 24/7, it's more having someone to model your behaviour on.

I was numb when my parents divorced, couldn't cope with it, went nuts, running wild. My brother, who's younger than me, got me through it. He was saying, 'We'll still see Dad,' and 'Maybe it's better than them arguing all the time.' He was six!

My dad and the rest of the family were surprised when I went down the acting route. I think they thought I'd amount to nothing – crap at school, police round the house every ten minutes, all that. When I dug myself out they were as surprised as everyone else and I don't think anyone knew how to help me. He could have helped me with how to cut in a piece of wallpaper.

I think the real father figure for me was Harold Pinter – even though he came into my life when I was older. Harold Pinter is the major British playwright of the twentieth century. If you've ever been on a drama course, you've studied him, if you've any education in theatre at all then you know who he is. He has his own style that's famous throughout the world. I had no fucking clue who he was when I met him.

It's high literature, the really brainy stuff. Now bearing in mind that I'm the kind of person who'd rather watch *You've Been Framed* than any Shakespeare, you might have thought we wouldn't get on. But we had a lot in common. We're both West Ham fans, both from East London. He started as an actor but found he was having more success in the writing game. Harold sounded very posh but in the days he was coming up, you had to lose the accent. I'd have been Donald Ducked then, wouldn't I?

So I hadn't a clue who he was when I met him, but he would turn out to be the most influential male figure in my life.

This ain't knocking my dad in any way. He left, so what? These things happen. You do what you gotta do. I could talk to my dad, sort of, but he had no idea about the theatre world or acting, which is where I wanted to be.

It is a bit of a laugh really. I went from thinking, 'I wish I had someone who knew a bit more about the old acting game to advise me,' to sitting in Harold Pinter's library with him telling me about life. It's like thinking, 'I'd like to learn tennis,' and having Roger Federer pop round your gaffe with his racket.

What I learned from Harold was there's no point mincing your words. If you've got something to say, say it.

He directed me in *Celebration* and *No Man's Land* and he was never one of these directors who say, 'Great, love, great, but if I could just make a tiny suggestion . . .' I've seen him reduce actors to tears – men and women. It didn't bother me, though. I'd rather an honest bollocking than someone making hints at you and talking about you behind your back.

That said, he was very supportive of me from the minute I met him. It was at an audition. I had an advantage because everyone else in there knew exactly who he was and they were shitting themselves.

I just came in, no small talk and said, 'Shall I crack on then, son?' He seemed to like it, thanked me and I heard on the way home I'd got the job. It was only then I began to realize who he was. I read a few of his plays and some of them I like, some of them I don't. To be honest I just don't understand some of the stuff. Other bits of it are very true to life.

I think we were friends for about five years. I used to go around his house, I'd talk about football, he'd go on about cricket, which means nothing to me. But I can't tell you what it does for your self-confidence, having someone like that believe in you. He treated me just like one of his equals.

He showed me that you should have confidence in your beliefs no matter where you come from. He's the only man I've heard of to turn down a knighthood, he hated all that shit. On most views me and him were very similar, having come from the same background. He was a lot more eloquent than me but you couldn't argue with what he had to say.

When critics get on your back, guttersnipes having a go at you saying you can't act, you've always got that inside you. 'Harold Pinter thought I could.' I'd always ask a critic who was having a go at me, in my head, 'How many Nobel Prizes have you got, you slag?'

I didn't understand all of his plays, I tried reading a few more but I got bored quite quickly. Most of it, though, I got it.

We didn't always see eye to eye when working together but I never felt afraid to let him know what I thought. Yes, he would occasionally bollock me but most of the time he was very supportive.

That's what I mean by him being a father figure to me. He's someone who I respected, showed love towards me, and whose love and regard propped me up through any storm. But he wasn't afraid to tell me when I was out of line. To be fair, Harold wasn't afraid to tell anyone when they were out of line. But that support, that ability to pull you up without crushing you, that's what it means to be a dad.

I really regret that I never got to say goodbye to him. When he died I was on a garage forecourt and I saw the headline on the front of *The Star*. I couldn't believe it, really couldn't believe it. I went weak. I wasn't invited to the funeral, but he knew so many important people who were rightly further up the invite list than me.

I'm grateful for every moment I spent with that man. He always knew the right thing to say at the right time. When I fucked up that time on stage, on Broadway, just forgot my lines, he was the best one, he snapped me out of it. He just said, 'Danny, it happens to the best of us.' And he touched me. He was very old school, he didn't touch people very much at all. He was not a tactile person. That reach-out to me, that touch on the arm was massive. Everyone else was saying, 'Were you drinking last night? Because you know it puts us in trouble as well.' That makes you sink into your seat even more. Don't get me wrong, I know it was a selfish act, but going on about it isn't going to improve my performance the next night.

He had bollocked me before but this time, he said, 'It's fine. Let's go and have a glass of wine.' And we did, we drank into the night. That's how he was a father figure – he had a lot of confidence in me and could transmit it to me.

I went from thinking, 'I wish I had someone who knew a bit more about the old acting game to advise me,' to sitting in Harold Pinter's library with him telling me about life. It's like thinking, 'I'd like to learn tennis,' and having Roger Federer pop round your gaffe with his racket.

Whenever I asked him for a note – a piece of advice on how I was performing something – he'd always say, 'Ask the author.' I'd say, 'You are the fucking author.' Then he'd say, 'Just do it. I don't need to tell you how to act, I will just tell you where to stand.' I'd think, 'Fine, you slag, I will never ask you another question again.' But then when I thought about it, it showed his trust in me.

There's a lot that he wrote that I still say to myself in my head. When I was doing his plays, I found it quite confusing, some of it. Now I've had a bit more time to reflect on it, it's part of me, a little gift he's given me. I find that incredible. Stuff like 'We have a clear obligation, which is to resist,' and 'A giggle and a cuddle, sometimes my ambitions extend no further than that.' 'Sometimes you're speaking to someone and you suddenly find you're another person.' It's almost as if I can hear him saying these things in my head.

My real dad compliments me so much now because he loves me on *EastEnders*. There's a reason for that – I take a lot from my dad and put it into the role I play. Not so much in the being a dad, because he was a bit shit in that respect, but Mick Carter has some of his mannerisms, some of the sayings he uses. When I have a break from the show, he's saying, 'You really are the best thing on that show, boy. I can't wait for you to come back on the screen.' He's now addicted to *EastEnders*. He never used to watch it at all, now he's watching it every night.

He wasn't exactly the arm around the shoulder sort when I was growing up. I used to play for his team and I missed a penalty once. He got the right hump. 'What you put it that side for? I told you to put it the other side. Use your mince pies!' I was gutted. There was no 'Don't worry about it son. Everyone makes mistakes under pressure.' He did what he thought was right, I'm not knocking him. I know he used to love watching me play football. And I used to love playing for him. They was good days.

I've got my own son, finally, and he's off his head. Nineteen months old, mental. The other day, we put him in his cot. There was a knock on the door from two girls. I thought maybe they wanted an autograph or something but they said there was a baby standing up at the bedroom window and they were worried he might climb out. I didn't even know he could get up that high. Luckily he hadn't worked out how to open it!

He was enjoying himself, having a right laugh. I nearly had a heart attack. Mind you, he's given me nightmares since before he was born.

The last three weeks of Jo's pregnancy were horrible, she kept getting these headaches that would lay her really low. She's diabetic so her blood sugar was all over the place. She tried to go for a natural birth but it weren't having it so she had to be rushed in for an emergency Caesarean.

Two days before I started *EastEnders* he was born.

This was the first kid I'd had that I thought, 'This could go wrong.' Childbirth's a worrying thing even if it's all going well, watching your missus go through it for six or seven hours isn't easy. You're watching this woman you love going through so much pain and what can you say? Nothing. It's an out-of-body experience. You have to hold her hand and say the right things. I wish I'd played Mick Carter back then because he was like the perfect birthing partner. I could have nicked some lines – not in a cynical way, but just to have something to comfort her.

So that's bad enough when things are going well.

With Arty I really thought, 'This kid could die.' He was premature, he came out weighing four pounds something, he was tiny. They had to keep testing to see if he was diabetic. It's horrible seeing your little baby being pricked with needles. They were sticking it in the bottom of his foot. They never seemed quite sure whether he was or he wasn't.

He had jaundice, so he was on a little sunbed. He was in the hospital for nearly two weeks, back and forth. It was a really weird time for me because I had to cement my place in that show really quickly. Otherwise it would have been a car crash and I wouldn't have lasted three months.

I wasn't around the first year nearly as much as I would have liked because I was filming. I was getting home in time to put a bottle in his mouth just before he went to bed. That first year was tough. He wouldn't come to me, he didn't know who I was. That kills you. It just means you have to put the work in later. My kids usually come to me when they're two or three anyway. They usually think of me as more fun and not the disciplinarian.

I had to work for the sake of the family so it took me a while to bond with Arty. Now we've had a bond up properly.

You have to sit back and be patient and bide your time early on, let the kids come to you. That was how it always used to be with kids anyway, years ago.

My dad's of the old school theory, never changed a nappy, never done a night feed, it just wasn't the done thing.

I don't think he really bonded with us before we were two or three either. If one of his kids was screaming, he couldn't have picked them up and comforted them. He'd have been rubbish. And obviously they would have felt that.

That hard work in the first year of *EastEnders* was all about the kids really. Being a father, to me, is the most important thing, it really makes me feel like I'm worth something. I had to succeed for them. His illness put a tremendous amount of pressure on me. He seemed so vulnerable, so in need of protection. Now he storms around like The Terminator – it's amazing to think he's the same kid that was lying there so sickly.

It's also been a challenge being a father to daughters. Sunnie's eight, still a kid, so it's a bit more straightforward. I love to get involved with her stuff at school. You have to be there for your kids. It's rewarding, there are bits I wouldn't miss for the world.

When she was doing this performance, singing 'Silent Night' in French I caught sight of her waiting in the wings to go on. I was gone, blubbing straight away. I looked around to see if any of the other people were crying. No. Just me then, the screen hard man. I had to turn away and pretend I was taking a phone call. This is why I don't have a nanny. Why would you want to hand that to someone else?

Dani is at a very difficult time for her – a teenager finding her way in the world. I can't really get my nut around the way a teenage girl thinks. All I can really do is give her love and affection. Some of the rubbish she moans about I can't understand – her weight, how she looks aesthetically, instead of working on what's important, which is the inside. That don't seem to matter to her. As long as she's got her hair and nails done and got a bit of a fake tan going on she thinks she's happy.

That's understandable at her age but I try to show her you've got to work from within and then slowly work on the other things. More than that, life is about fulfilling your potential, being all you can be for its own sake, not because it buys you a holiday in Tenerife and gets you to the front of a queue in a nightclub.

I do trust her though, because I know she's a very loving girl who has come on this incredible journey with me and her mum. It must have been a big adjustment for her, coming out of the East End, moving to suburban Essex and a private school where no one talks like her.

I know she's got her head screwed on right and I think she'll do OK in the end. By OK, I mean that she'll be a happy and fulfilled person who gives the best of herself to life and gets the satisfaction of doing that. I can't stand over her, make her mistakes for her or stop her making them. It can't all be roses.

We bounce through life having great times, beautiful times and horrific dark times. That's a guarantee. If everything was like the Disney Channel, family life would be boring. You need the bad times to appreciate the good ones.

And there have been dark times in the family recently. When you get near forty, people start dying around you – you start losing nans, mums and dads. You start looking down at your own kids, thinking about when they're grown up and it's your turn to go. It's a strange period of your life.

I do like getting older, getting that bit wiser. It makes me a better person, and it makes me a better actor because obviously acting's about drawing on experiences. You can understand situations a little bit more, you become more the thinker as you get older.

I've always been someone who thinks a lot about life. I've been able to give Dani some advice. When she comes out of a relationship, she sometimes wants to go full throttle into a new one. I can sit back and say, 'You need to find out who you are.'

That's the most difficult thing. It doesn't matter what anyone else says or thinks, you need to know who you are inside. Don't worry about giving someone a perception of you, or worrying about what you think they want to see, concentrate on who you are. That takes time, it's pain and it's joy and everything in between. When you know who you are, you can start taking these decisions about falling in love and things like that. You need to know who is right for you, which is the right circle of people for you and to do that you need to know who you are inside.

To an extent, we never really answer that question. We're always putting little spins on ourselves – I'm a different person at work to the person I am in front of my nan with dementia and I'm a different person again in front of Sunnie's teacher to the one I am when talking to a policeman.

So what do I want for my kids?

Just to take joy in what they do and to see them make a contribution to the world, whether that's as a dustman or head of the United Nations. That's a major part of being a dad, helping them to do that.

6

They say women are from Venus, men are from Mars. To me it's like women are from Stoke Newington . . . men are from Custom House.

You might laugh, but I think it's important to be in touch with your emotions and I think of myself as a bit of a sensitive soul. It's an essential part of being an actor.

For instance, I can cry quite easily if I have to. One of the things I sometimes use is to remember my little dog Sam – like the littlest hobo, with his question-mark tail.

He lived in the days when dogs could just roam the streets, none of this shit you have nowadays where you have to keep 'em locked up. Why is that? Traffic, I suppose, but I think a dog should be free.

We just opened the door in the morning and off he'd go with his little gang of mates. I'd be out with my mates and we'd see each other throughout the day – he'd be strolling past with a burger in his gob, I'd give him a nod and we'd crack on. He was amazing – he would wait for the zebra crossing, everything.

I often think men can express their softer feelings around dogs better than they can around people sometimes. Why is that? There are blokes that will sit hugging a dog watching the TV who would never do that with their missus.

Maybe men see more of themselves in the dog than they do in their partners. A dog's just Homer Simpson in a furry suit, really, isn't he, and I think he appeals to that uncomplicated, straightforward side of a bloke.

I would love a dog now but it's Jo who would have to look after it, because I'm filming a lot. Definitely more of a dog man than a cat man. I mean, I don't mind house cats but would you see a lion acting bollocky and blanking you because you ain't putting any tuna out? Jo doesn't like animals – nothing that breathes in the house, she says. That said, she goes around on a horse, so that breathes don't it?

I've got the dog in The Vic, Lady Di. It hates me, gives me evils when it looks at me. It don't like many people, to be honest. Bulldogs shouldn't be actors. They're too lazy. I've had scenes with babies – who are very unpredictable – and a dog that hates me. It don't get no worse.

We used to have Tramp on set and he was incredible. I tell you, that dog was so well trained. It had a cravat, it could make you a cup of tea. It was like you put a fag in your mouth and this little paw would reach up with a lighter in it. It was a shame when he got wrote out because I liked him a lot.

It sounds a bit sick but a dog never asks you to change, or challenges you like a person does. Food, water, walk, nice place to sleep, vet when he's ill, that's him sorted. Happy. He's never going to ask you to express what you're really feeling inside. I'm not saying that makes them better than people, because of course it don't. It's just that your relationship is uncomplicated in a way it can never be with a woman.

Men are happy to relate to each other like dogs. Obviously, we skip the arse sniffing, well most of us do, but when I remember little Sam and his mates cruising Custom House, I'm reminded of the way me and my mates relate to each other. We stand up for each other, we love each other but our main thing is having a laugh. A Staff's not going to turn to a Collie and say, 'What are you really feeling when you're pissing up that post? I hate it when you won't share with me.'

This isn't to say we don't have emotions, of course we do. I was really upset by my dog's death, massively. But I don't feel the need to go on about it all the time, or to share that. For me, it's something I carry inside me and assume no other fucker is particularly interested in.

Women sometimes expect the heart-to-heart from men and I do find that hard. Sometimes Jo asks me to do that, says, 'Let's sit down for a girly gossip.' That's one of her favourite expressions but it makes me feel like a dog – just after its owner's found the sofa ripped to bits. I freeze.

I know I shouldn't but it's just that blokes aren't designed to talk about their feelings. If they go out together they talk bollocks with each other – sport, jokes, all that. Talking about our feelings just don't come naturally to us. Maybe in the future it will.

They say women are from Venus, men are from Mars. To me it's like women are from Stoke Newington – Victorian houses, wholefood shops, jazz cafés, cashback at the foot spa and worried about litter on the high street, all that. Men are from Custom House. Flats, four betting shops in a street, a chip shop, a couple of boozers and that's all.

Do we have any deep feelings we can unearth? Well some, but I sense she isn't asking me to start laying it on her about when my granddad died or something like that. It's something else she's after and I'm not sure she can even say what it is. When Jo asks me to give a glimpse into my inner life I feel like a 1980s North Welsh shopkeeper when someone comes in and asks for goji berries. I want to help but I really don't know what they're on about. I'll go in the back and dig out a packet of Fishermen's Friends, see if they'll do.

It's like that if we have a row. Jo will sit indoors thinking about it, I'll just go out and forget about it.

I think it's a primeval thing. In the old days men would be out hunting and running around after antelope and whatever, women would be in by the fire, looking after the kids and talking.

Men do have very deep feelings but they tend to be a bit more about tribal identity – football, the area you're from, than, er, whatever the other stuff is. Of course, we do feel love. Love to me is when you're excited by all the little things your partner does, the way they move, little expressions on their face, all that. At the start you're wary of each other, thinking, 'Should I call? Have I called too many times?' But then you start to see them bloom as a person, not just an idea you have in your nut.

Men do have very deep feelings but they tend to be a bit more about tribal identity – football, the area you're from, than, er, whatever the other stuff is.

For a man, and for a woman, love is bound up with feelings of intense jealousy. That is one feeling I wish I could stop myself expressing. I do feel jealous if I see Jo talking to another bloke, maybe sitting on someone's knee at a party. I know it's harmless, completely harmless – I'm there, for God's sake, but I do feel a bit of a stirring. I appreciate it's my problem, something for me to deal with and I can't be putting that on her.

Similarly, she struggles with jealousy, I know. Because of who I am, I'm of interest to a lot of women. I'm not stupid enough to think that's just because of my charm or good looks – people often confuse actors with their roles. I think women are attracted to Mick Carter or one of the naughty boys I've played in film, rather than to me. I mean, look at me, I'm not exactly gonna get a call if they do *Magic Mike 3* am I?

Still, Jo can't help but feel that attention I get and I can't help feeling jealous about her. It's a bad thing in some ways and can lead to rows but it's a bond between us. Let's be clear, though, there's a limit. I'm not one of these geezers who's checking where she is every ten minutes or losing it if she talks to another man, or even has male friends. That's love, the balance of jealousy and trust. If I didn't feel jealous, I wouldn't feel I loved her but I wouldn't love her if I allowed that jealousy to fence her in.

You know if you're in love because you take that feeling of jealousy you have inside you and you stamp it down a bit for the other person. That's an example of a feeling it's better not to share, if you can help it.

This, of course, is also a problem for men. We're not always aware of our gentler feelings, or aren't able to put them into words. We don't have that problem with anger. We can put that into words very easily indeed. However, when my fiancée asks what I'm thinking, I doubt she wants to hear about all the people I'd like to kick up the arse.

There's also days I can't be bothered with doing the small talk. I can't be fucked. I respect anyone who has the bollocks to just not do any of all that.

There are definitely times when we men could do with looking at our emotions a bit more clearly, or just being able to accept them. When my granddad was dying, I was the only bloke in the family who could bear to be with him.

My dad, for instance, never came to see him when he was in his final illness because he said he wanted to remember him how he was – big lad, former boxer, merchant seaman with the tattoos – rather than the bag of bones he'd become. My dad was very close to my granddad, even though granddad was my mum's dad.

I understood that, but it made me feel quite angry. What they really meant was they couldn't stand it because they might cry and that, to them, was the most terrible thing on earth.

Bollocks, we all cry sometimes. I can well up at kids' films, so I ain't got a problem with it in front of my granddad. I wish my dad and the other blokes in the family could have turned that around, seen crying as a sign of the strength of their emotion.

I don't blame them personally, not at all. It's just how they was brought up. I've got a bit of that, only less than they have. I hope Arty will have less than me.

You can take it too far, though. They're big feelings around grief and death and easy to recognize for anyone. Sometimes, I wonder about the smaller things. I think blokes have such deep defences that sometimes they don't even know they have them feelings. And that's the worry, when the missus asks you to open your heart for her. You can't even do it for yourself. Surely, there's no reason why you should if you're cracking on fine without it. Why not just let these feelings simmer away and eventually disappear without ever coming to your mind? I really don't see why you have to go raking around looking for something to feel miserable about.

I know that sounds rough but my generation of men just aren't well prepared for this sort of thing and, to be fair, a lot of us are happy that way.

I sometimes wonder if it would be good for blokes' dads to prepare 'em with things to say when women ask them to express their feelings. I wish someone had told me. Do you just say 'vulnerable' – I know some of them like to hear that, unless you actually are feeling vulnerable, in which case they'll see you as weak and do for ya. Women can be like sharks if they sense blood.

If you say you're feeling great, they sometimes don't take that as enough. What to say to close down the conversation as quickly as humanly possible? Turning it back's a good idea – 'I'm OK, but what's on *your* mind?' Then you can just tune out and nod while they go on. I'm not pretending to have the answers.

If that's not hard enough, there are other questions women can spring on you at any moment that can really smash you up if you're not prepared. 'Why do you love me?' That's another one that makes you feel like you're a kid, nipping out of Woolworths with a couple of bags of pick 'n' mix shoved up your jumper when you feel the hand of the store detective on your shoulder.

What do they want? A list?

If I get an hour to think of all the reasons I love Jo I can quite easily put it down on paper. But there's something about having the person in front of you, combined with the fact they may have just been giving it you in the ear about some shit, that makes it very difficult to reply to on the spot.

You can't say, 'Leave it out, treacle, I've got a bad head.' That might enrage them.

How about 'You complete me'? No. Then they might get the idea you have something missing. You're caught in a balancing act with women. On the one hand they want you to be the sensitive type and on the other they want you to be strong and self-reliant. Say 'You complete me' and that will go in the book for next time you have a row. 'You shouldn't look to me to prop you up!' You know the drill.

Don't, for God's sake, say something like, 'I'm here, aren't I, living with ya!' I've never tried that one but I know blokes who have and it yields no good results.

The thing is, we don't get the practice at this sort of question. If I go out with my mates they don't ask me why I like them. And if they did, I'd say, 'I don't,' and they'd find that funny and that would be the end of it.

I can't provide any answers, here, just flag up the questions.

Women are a puzzle, for sure. They are a beautiful puzzle, they test us, they help us grow. I just wish they wouldn't try to help me grow halfway through *Soccer AM* by asking, 'What are you thinking?' I'm normally thinking something like, 'West Ham are going to get killed this season if they don't spend some money.'

7

*One minute I'm down on my luck, driving at
fifty on the North Circular to keep the fuel consumption down, the next I'm looking at a dream
come true.*

For me, a major part of being a dad is putting the
dinner on the table, at least that was what I was
brought up to believe. I think women have every
right to absolute equality with men, no question.
There is still a bit of me, though, that would be
uncomfortable if it was my missus who was going
out earning and me that was at home with the kids.
Nothing wrong with doing that for a bit, and there
are times I've had to.

This makes me realize that being at home with kids
is the hardest job in the world, certainly much tougher
than what I do. But you can take the boy out of the
East End and all that, but you can't take the East End
out of the boy. I was brought up traditional and a little
bit of that is still in my nut saying, 'You're a bloke,
you're the breadwinner.' That's just how I feel, I'm not
trying to tell no one else what to do.

Of course that's all cushty until you ain't the bread-winner any more.

It's a pressure to be in an up-and-down career like acting if you have it fixed in your mind that it's up to you to come up with the family wedge.

Plenty of people in plenty of jobs have that, of course – there are few stable earners any more. But it's affected me at times when I have been what's known as 'resting' – out of work and boracic to the rest of us.

Acting's very unpredictable. Just before I got the *EastEnders* job I wasn't getting much work. I'd had a couple of good films but not massive earners and suddenly the old blower stops ringing. I have no idea why it goes this way. The ten years before I'd been working day and night. All of a sudden I can't get arrested. Why does that happen? I wish I knew. Anyway, things were looking a bit iffy and we had notices from bailiffs once or twice.

This makes you feel you're failing not just as an actor but as a dad and as a man. I'm not lazy, I like working and I like feeling I'm doing right by my family.

I thought I was looking at *Celebrity Big Brother* and then God knows what. I can't do anything else but act. Never take nothing for granted because even when you're riding high, you're only ever a breath away from selling *The Big Issue*.

Big Brother came knocking on my door, they thought I'd be perfect for them but I just didn't think I could do it. To me, it's such a full stop on your career. It's an admission that you're skint and need money.

That said, I can't say it hasn't been tempting. If you get thrown out in the first week then it's a decent wedge for a week's work. But it's a kick in the nuts to the ego – out of twelve celebrities, you're the least popular. When you're already down, it could feel like the final blow.

I'm glad I swerved in the end.

Why did the film roles dry up? It was my fault really, I was just saying 'yes' to everything. I wasn't listening to agents and I wasn't listening to managers. To me it was all about a pound note, putting my kids' dinner on the table.

It was the kids that kept me going. If I've done anything right in my life it's them three. They keep me positive, they're a credit to us. I was determined to get back on it again for them. You want them to look up to you, to be inspired by you.

I'd do one day on a film without telling anyone. I didn't have a contract to do it, so I had no control over it but if it was only a day it didn't seem much to me. The next thing I know they've put my face on the cover and it's shit. You can get away with one or two of them but no more.

You have three or four on the spin then you lose all your credibility and, as quickly as it comes, it goes.

You get all these other kids coming out of drama school and while you're having a bad period someone is really hot. They're always going to go for the hot person, no matter that you might be better for the role. It hurts. Then a film comes out you did a year ago. You'd forgotten all about it and it's pony.

Then you're in this weird world because you need to promote it in order for it to earn numbers. If you don't promote it it's less likely to be a success. You want to turn your back on it but you can't.

Mind you, the last film I had out smashed it. It was called *Assassin*. It was with Martin and Gary Kemp. It did really well and it only had £12,000 promotion budget.

The film before that, *Vendetta* was a massive success, it's up to 600,000 units now. I'm playing an action hero, a mini Jason Statham moment. I put everything into it. I think I'm a better actor than Jason Statham, though he's got a much better body than me and probably has a better look to be an action hero.

But after that, nothing. Weird, eh?

It was the kids that kept me going. If I've done anything right in my life it's them three. They keep me positive, they're a credit to me. I was determined to get back on it again for them. You want them to look up to you, to be inspired by you.

When they said they'd got me an *EastEnders* job, to be honest, I wouldn't have gone if it hadn't been for the family. I thought I'd be in it for ten minutes but it would be money. I'd run around the Square three months and then be blown up in a car by Phil.

One of my big anxieties going to the meeting was whether I'd have enough petrol in the motor to make it there. Seriously, it was that bad. I'm driving there in a Porsche, worried I'm gonna run out of fuel and not have enough money to fill it up. That's my insane life.

Dominic Treadwell-Collins, who is the Executive Producer of *EastEnders*, chose me at my lowest ebb and I'll always be grateful to him for that. He brought me in and I thought, 'Here we go, short contract playing a gangster.' But no! He sat me down on me throne and tells me how brilliant I am, and how he'd read an interview about me being brought up by women and how he wanted me to take over The Queen Vic, which has never been done in its history by an incoming character. I thought, 'Wow.'

He explained the role to me and I thought, 'Well, he gets me.' I played it down, told him I'd think about it, not wanting to look too desperate.

I got out of that meeting turning cartwheels and was straight on the phone to Jo shouting, 'We're saved! We're saved!' I was thumping the steering wheel, at the same time hoping I'd have enough juice in the tank to make it back. A weird situation indeed. Sometimes my life surprises even me.

One minute I'm down on my luck, driving at fifty on the North Circular to keep the fuel consumption down, the next I'm looking at a dream come true. I can't tell you how I love the role of Mick Carter. It's perfect for me – exactly what I wanted, a chance to show a bit more than just the hard man, to do a bit of a comic turn, show a bit of vulnerability.

Still, even as I took it, there was a little bit inside me that was afraid. I knew it would be difficult for me but more so for my family. I knew the press would go over my life with a magnifying glass, digging out all the dirt they could. The thing is, even by then, I had changed and grown up. We'd put the past behind us but this might stir it all up again.

8

Given what I know of hooligans – which is more than most considering I've done two TV series chasing 'em about – they ain't actually all that different to each other. Most of 'em would be top pals had they been born three streets to the east or west.

Football hooliganism gets a bad press, and rightly I suppose. This is the twenty-first century and it's not acceptable to run around in a firm like it used to be. So it's bad, all right? We accept that now. Debate over.

However, as with a lot of things, there's a case of double standards operating here. It gets grief out of all proportion to the harm it causes.

The main reason it gets such a bad name nowadays is that it's not part of the culture of the people who write the newspapers and work for the TV companies, all that.

For them, it's OK to charge about the country after a fox and set dogs on it. It's not OK to meet with another firm and knock the pony out of each other, no matter that you've both agreed to do that. Nobody rings the fox up a week before the meet and says, 'Oi,

Basil Brush. Bring ya top boys,' do they? No. He's sitting at home enjoying ten minutes with his family watching reruns of Tommy Walsh's *Eco House* or whatever foxes do and the next thing he knows he's got 200 beagles wrapped round his alderman's nail.

But, to hear what some people have got to say, you'd think that was OK. Foxhunting's always gone on, they say. You won't stop it even if you legislate against it. Aren't these arguments sounding familiar? That's what I'd say about hooliganism, and drugs for that matter. But because they're applied to something enjoyed by Prince Charles rather than down The Prince Charles, they're suddenly worth listening to.

Is football hooliganism the worst thing in the world? I don't think so.

If the Berkeley Hunt or whoever goes running through your allotment chasing a fox – which happens, believe me – then it's 'Sorry, Squire, here's a couple of quid,' and the Old Bill have a jolly good laugh about it. You get the ICF (Inter City Firm, associated with West Ham) chasing some other firm across there and you'd see a right different reaction. There'd be three riot vans and half a dozen news teams over there smartish.

Look, I'm not condoning firms having a tear-up, particularly when they do it around kids or families looking for a day out at the football. I'm glad it's gone from the grounds, largely, now – though it does take a bit of an edge off the game. Actually, given what I know of hooligans – which is more than most considering I've done two TV series chasing 'em about – they ain't actually all that different to each other. Most of 'em would be top pals had they been born three streets to the east or west.

Take the violence out and you've got a positive thing in the hooligan group. They're quite accepting. You take Cass Pennant, the old West Ham hooligan. He was a black man adopted by a white family in the East End at a time when there weren't too many black faces about. He was in with people who might have given him grief if they'd met him in the street. When he was with the firm, they didn't see his colour – he was just Claret and Blue.

I met some interesting people – some of the hooligans are surprisingly intelligent, though to be honest a lot of them are exactly as thick as you imagine.

It's heartwarming in a way.

Because I did two TV series on hooligans, people often think I admire them. This ain't so. People saw the sort of roles I was playing back then and thought

I'd be a good presenter. To be honest, I wasn't all that interested until they told me how much they'd be paying.

I met some interesting people – some of the hooligans are surprisingly intelligent, though to be honest a lot of them are exactly as thick as you imagine.

And this is the point – if they weren't beating the beans out of each other, they'd be doing it to someone else. You might say it's a sort of safety valve that stops these individuals exploding.

So, like I say, it's not a good thing at all and the Old Bill can't ignore it. But is it the worst thing in the world like it's made out to be? I don't think so.

9

*I'm standing there, looking at some lemurs, smoth-
ered to death in an over-tight kid's zebra mask and I
think, 'How did it turn out like this? Is this normal?'*

I never wanted to be famous, ever, and I think anyone
who does want to be famous must need their nut looking at.

I wanted to be an actor and fame is a sort of byprod-
uct of that. If you're going to be successful at this game
then you can't avoid fame.

However, I've always been uncomfortable with it.
Don't get me wrong, there's stuff I like about it –
getting invited nice places, free trainers and all the rest
but there's plenty I don't.

My problem is partly that – in this country – I've
got a level of fame approaching David Beckham but I
don't live in Beckingham Palace. I live in a normal
house on a normal estate. My neighbours are ordinary
working people, not pop stars. I don't move around
only in posh restaurants and hang about with Elton
John. I go down the local carvery with my family. All
you can eat! Let's put it this way, they never made no

money out of me! I went in there like a swarm of locusts.

You wouldn't believe how mad the fame thing can be. I was driving down the A406 the other day and there's a bloke driving but hanging out of his car window taking photos of me. I was saying, 'Look at the road mate! I don't want to die.' It's insane.

Let me be clear, I love people being interested in me, I love that they dig what I do so much, absolutely love it. But there are times when I wish I could turn it all off for half an hour and nip down the pie and mash shop and be quiet on my own.

The attention that I get, I can never quite under-stand. It's really flattering but at the same time it's puzzling. What is it that I bring out in people? Some people seem amazed I'm in front of them. I've had people burst into tears. It's a real moment for both of us but right in my soul I don't get it. I'm only me. I'm nothing special – ask my missus.

When you've been filming on a freezing beach for three hours – as I was earlier this year in Southend – all you want to do is get in the haddock and bugger off, but you can't. I cannot do it. I'm really aware it's my fans who put me where I am. So I have photos with all of them, every last one. I can't have a photo with some of them and then drop the others out.

Just a note: there's a new trend at the moment where people like to just shove babies at you. Some of them have pissy nappies. The babies are very nice but I do prefer a clean one.

It's easy to start to feel slightly strange about it and like everyone's got an agenda, which I know they haven't. You can get paranoid. I can see why George Michael's become a recluse. Obviously I'm not comparing myself to George Michael, and, to be fair, he did get caught wanking in a khazi. That's on another level.

A while back I started to get a bit anxious with the sheer level of scrutiny I was under – people with smartphones everywhere, the paps trying to crawl up my arse every time I went out the house. Maybe I was paranoid, maybe I wasn't but it's how I felt. Joanne was having Arty and had been diagnosed as diabetic. In the same week she is going to give birth, I'm starting on *EastEnders*, the biggest job of my life.

So, like anyone, I'm flesh and blood, I'm worried about Joanne, worried about the job, worried about Arty. I feel like just taking a few weeks off until Joanne is OK but I can't. This is my family's future here, and

> *There's a new trend at the moment where people like to just shove babies at you. Some of them have pissy nappies. The babies are very nice but I do prefer a clean one.*

there are no second chances if you make a pig's ear of it at your first go.

This starts to really get on top of me – the pressure of the long days, being away from the family at such a tough time, the feeling that I really need to succeed. I've taken a gamble, come from film to soap. If I don't make this the best performance ever, which is what I aim for, then it could be goodnight Danny, *Celebrity Big Brother*, then sign on, son. It starts to freak my nut out. On the one hand, things are going brilliantly – I've got a new son, an amazing opportunity with *EastEnders*, but my son isn't well and the whole thing feels like it's on the edge of a cliff and I might fall off at any minute.

I knew it would become more difficult to do the normal everyday things that you take for granted. I went to the zoo with my daughter a while back and everyone was chasing us about so I had to put on a zebra mask they had in the shop. The thing was it was for kids and was really tight, so I kept thinking I'd pass out. Still, we got to see the animals OK, so it was worth it but when I'm standing looking there, at some lemurs, smothered to death in an over-tight kid's zebra mask, I think, 'How did it turn out like this? Is this normal?'

I had a picture in my mind of me being found unconscious outside the lemurs, a zebra mask cutting off my breathing. It's like something from a dream.

There have been amazing things about fame though, things I feel really privileged to have been involved in. I got a call from a family whose daughter had been in a car crash and was in a coma. She was a big fan of mine so they asked me if I'd go down and talk to her. To be honest, I was in two minds about it. I didn't think it would do any good and I also thought it would be upsetting for me and for the family when nothing happened.

Anyway, I got down there and the family were lovely and I just sat with her and talked to her. She woke up! I could not believe it. She got better really quickly as well and could talk. I got a little bit overcome by the whole thing and ended up crying my eyes out in the car on the way home. Obviously it made me feel really good to be able to do something like that and made the rest of the shit that comes with being famous worth it. We're friends on Twitter still and she just got married.

Also, I'm not going to lie, the money doesn't hurt. I'm not as well off as many people think but I'm still doing better than I ever have done. I'm just about to move into my dream house, if the legal side of things ever works out. It's got a little annex which I'm turning into The Queen Vic. The prop boys are going to come in and build a mini version of it for me. I've already nicked an old sign they had. *EastEnders* has played a massive part in my life and it can be a little bit of a man cave for me.

10

If Liam Neeson says there are ghosts, there are fucking ghosts.

Are there really ghosts? Of course there are. There are hundreds of the melts knocking about. They have been around since anyone can remember and there are thousands of stories and accounts to back up their existence.

People all over the world see them. There's even cave paintings of ghosts – though I suppose they could just have faded a bit. That was a joke, all right.

If the legacy of the ages were not enough to convince you, I have seen a ghost myself. I have had to suffer some diabolical piss-taking over this, but I swear it on my life.

I'd gone out tagging with a mate of mine. I was aged about fourteen and we had a load of pens and spray cans to mark up the trains that were in the depot in Stratford Yard.

You had to bunk over a wall to get in and go under this long alleyway. As we were heading towards the trains, this monk, in full monk's clobber, hood, rope round his waist, the lot, comes walking towards us.

Naturally I shat a brick but I was too scared even to run away. I just kept walking, kept me nut down and he went past us. When he'd gone by, I said to my mate, 'Did you see that?' He said he had. When we turned round for a pipe, the ghost geezer had gone. Vanished into thin air. It couldn't have gone through the wall.

Henry Stapp is one of science's top boys. He is a quantum mechanics bloke – quantum mechanics being nothing to do with cars but about a sort of nosebleed physics.

I looked it up later and there used to be a monastery on the site – Stratford Langthorne Abbey – also known as West Ham Abbey. I'm not going to claim the ghost was a West Ham fan, though I suppose being able to walk through walls would be valuable for nicking into the games. He was wearing white, not Claret and Blue anyway. I hope he wasn't Spurs, not on our manor.

There's been sightings of a monk's ghost there before – and I never knew about that until I started researching this book.

On the Newham Story website – which collects stories from the manor – there's a thing by an old lady who remembers being told about a ghostly white monk that suddenly disappeared into a tunnel – exactly what happened to us. I went cold when I read that.

The website says:

> There are lots of rumours of tunnels in Newham, and if all were true the borough by now would have sunk into them, but there were moats in and around the area of the Abbey, and if you cover a moat, what do you get, a tunnel, and the Cistercian Monks in the Abbey were known as the 'White' monks because of their white habits!

Now tell me I was dreaming it!

Who was it? I don't know but I tell you this, we got out of there lively – dropped the pens and cans and got home as quick as we could.

I was on the Jonathan Ross show with Liam Neeson and he said he'd seen a ghost too. He was going back from a dance at four in the morning – stone cold sober – and on this bridge called 'Maggie's Bridge' he saw the ghost of this Maggie moving across. If Liam Neeson says there are ghosts, there are fucking ghosts.

The thing about ghosts is this – you say you've seen them and half the people will laugh at you. The other half will say they've seen one too. They can't all be liars, can they?

Jo has had experiences with this. She gets an achy arm and feels it's her granddad putting his hand on her.

I swear to God my house is haunted – even though it's a new build. I don't know if it's built on something weird or what but I'm sure there's a ghost in Dani's bedroom. There is a weird feel to the gaffe.

I've had a couple of people stay over and sleep in that room, and they've all said there's something strange about it. Danny-Boy Hatchard, who plays my son in *EastEnders*, stayed over and he left first thing in the morning because the room freaked him out.

I asked him why he left after a few hours, and he said there was this knocking. Knock, knock, knock. I said it's probably a pipe, but he went, 'Nah, it weren't a pipe.'

Dani was in there listening to music and she heard someone shouting her name.

Weird shit, and no mistake.

I don't think programmes like *Most Haunted* have done much for ghosts. Especially when Derek Acorah said he got messages about Madeleine McCann, that she's going to be reincarnated. I hope, if Derek's reincarnated, he comes back as himself as punishment.

There's lots of explanations for what ghosts might be. Some say they are hallucinations caused by changes in the earth's magnetic field. Some say they might be caused by hormonal changes in the body. There are other explanations that say they might be inter-dimensional beings or clouds of weird matter acting in ways we don't understand. Maybe they are aliens, come here to study us, taking a moody form so as not to get sussed.

When I say they're real, just like with the aliens, science is right behind me. Dr Henry Stapp is one of science's top boys. He is a quantum mechanics bloke – quantum mechanics being nothing to do with cars but about a sort of nosebleed physics. I tried to read his theory but to be honest, it's a right mindfuck and I lost my way after about three lines. He believes in ghosts anyway and thinks they're just the energy of the dying brain escaping into the universe.

Then there's Dr Peter Fenwick. This geezer is a top brain doctor at places like the Maudsley psychiatric hospital and Broadmoor. He says the mind may be independent of the brain. When the body dies, it fucks off to carry on having it.

Having weighed it all up, I think the most likely explanation is that ghosts are spirits of the dead. Why would so many people see the same thing at the site of famous hauntings? Why would these things cling to places associated with the dead?

I can understand why people are sceptical. There's not enough pictures of ghosts for my liking – I would like to see more that you could trust. The problem, I suppose, is that cameras have always been a little bit iffy, haven't they? Even if you've got a good snap of a ghost, there's always the chance it could be a fake, even more in these days of Photoshop.

I want to believe in ghosts, though. It would mean some of the people I love who have died might still be around.

I always thought my granddad would come back and see me. I nursed him through his final illness with cancer and we had a right bond-up. I'd sit rolling him spliffs and we'd just talk about all sorts of stuff. We'd talk a lot about acting. I'd got the agent, done *Prime Suspect*, but he died before it aired, which was gutting. I know he'd have been so proud of me.

I was very close to him and I expected him to come back to visit me. I don't know why he hasn't. I would love him to.

It doesn't bother me that we have to die, only that it sometimes takes so long.

I don't think I'm afraid of death. When you're gone, you're gone, you don't know nothing about it. I am afraid of getting ill and old, though – not just having a few lines on your face, but when you get so old life's not really worth living any more.

It doesn't bother me that we have to die, only that it sometimes takes so long.

When the spark has gone, when the light inside isn't there, why are we kept hanging on, this set of failing organs, this bag of bones and breath? I never want to be like that.

My granddad looked terrible at the last. He was one of these blokes who would never go to the doctor's. He'd had difficulty pissing, said nothing. Eventually, when it gets so bad he can't go, he goes to the doctor's and it's too late.

I find it very weird how it picks certain people and not others. You can be the healthiest person in the world, go to the gym, drink your aloe vera juice and, bang, cancer of the little finger, it spreads and you're dead in a year. And yet Gary Glitter lives. Work that out.

My nan on my dad's side has dementia. There's this weird thing about life. You start off as a baby, just curious about everything, everything is fascinating, even the washing machine, then, you're this innocent ball of energy. And then you live your life, and you become a child again, and this is what dementia has done to my nan. She is herself for about five minutes, and then she switches into this weird child-like mode where you almost feel you have to pat her on the head and say, 'Well done, well done.' She says the most random shit, the most trippy shit about a pigeon living in her wheelchair. She asks you if you've met the pigeon yet, and I humour her because it's a tricky thing. I say, 'Yes, it's a lovely pigeon,' and then she is happy.

She refuses to call my little boy Arty. She says, 'Why have you called him Arty? People will call him Arty Farty. I want you to call him Marshall.' I've never heard of a Marshall other than Marshall Mathers, Eminem, so I don't mind that, but it's not his name. She thinks he will be bullied at school. I try to say to her, 'Well, my name's Danny. Danny Fanny,' but she will not have it.

It's this dementia that's kicked in. She gave me a teddy and keeps asking, 'Does Marshall like it?' Of course, he does like it, and I tell her so. Again and again. It's very sad.

In these homes you have these levels of age and illness. They start off on level 1 and they sit in their little lounge, watching TV, they make cards and they listen to old music. They're a bit gone in the head but they can have conversations. Then you go up a floor and they're all just sitting in a room, drugged up to the eyeballs, shitting and pissing themselves, sort of with it but not at all. Then on the third floor, that's where you're just awaiting death. It's hard to think about.

I go to that home and it absolutely kills me. It really hurts me to see my nan in there but I also think, 'This is what we've got to look forward to.'

I don't want to get to that stage, I'd rather be ironed out than sitting there waiting to go on that third floor. There's a couple of women I know in there and you ask, 'Where's Maude?' They say, 'Oh, she's gone up a floor.' It's difficult to deal with. I suppose, with my nan, we're just waiting for her to get moved up a floor, dreading it.

We lost my granddad recently. He was eighty-four. My nan had a stroke about five years ago. So he lost his wife there. My nan was a very well-kept woman, always turned out well. She'd sit there, rolling her Golden Virginia up all into neat little snouts and she'd put them in a cute little cigarette case. She has a stroke, can't walk any more, can't go to the toilet on her own. My granddad has to wipe her arse, has to feed her, bathe her. Downstairs there was a hoist to lift her up. He put up with this five years and eventually she had to go into a home because he just couldn't do it any more. This was because of his age and also I think it took a massive emotional toll on him. So in she goes.

Then he goes to visit her every day. One day, he got dressed to go and see her, obviously felt a bit tired so he set an alarm, lay down on the settee fully dressed and he died. My dad found him, the alarm was still going off. He was curled up, obviously not in pain and I just feel he gave up. He had a mini heart attack in his sleep. We all assumed it was going to be my nan who went first. He was still going fishing, he was a big man, good head of hair on him and he just died. I think it all got too much for him and he sort of gave up, just ran out of steam.

This is the thing with dying, it doesn't always come clean and simple, at a happy time. You get tested, big style, before you peg out. If my nan hadn't been so ill, would my granddad still be here today? I think so, I really do.

The human condition, ageing, heaps an awful lot of grief on us before we go. That's why I'm not too fussed about looking after my health, trying to live forever. I'd rather peg it from a heart attack when I'm sixty-five, having had a laugh, than spend a life smoking menthol fags to keep my lungs clean and face a slow and depressing end.

We deal with grand-dad's death, which is heavy in itself but then we have to go and tell my nan who's got dementia that he's gone. She's expecting him to walk through the door at any minute. So to break the news to someone that their husband's gone after fifty-five years of marriage is very hard.

Well, she's not having it. We tell her, she takes

You can be the healthiest person in the world, go to the gym, drink your aloe vera juice and, bang, cancer of the little finger, it spreads and you're dead in a year. And yet Gary Glitter lives. Work that out.

it on board, cries and then five minutes later she says, 'What time is John coming? I know he's not dead, he's in the lounge.'

It's a heartbreaking situation. Would she be better off dead? Maybe. I think there's something quite blissful about death if you're in a great deal of pain. Now obviously, I'm not encouraging anyone to commit suicide but I think it would be a release if she went, if there is anything on the other side.

She says, 'Do you know what, Dan?' – though some-times she calls me Tony because she mistakes me for my dad – 'I wake up and I sob my heart out because I didn't die in the night.' That's a truthful, honest state-ment. Obviously I would be devastated if she went, but you just think, 'Maybe, just maybe, she should be allowed to go. It might be a beautiful thing for her.' It would break my heart to lose her but what kind of life is she living now?

It's difficult to form a view on assisted dying. On the one hand I think we withhold from people a kindness we extend to dogs. If your dog's on his last legs, ill and sick with no chance of recovery, you have him put down to save him pain.

A person doesn't get that choice. But it's difficult – would my nan feel that she had to take that option to save everyone the bother of looking after her? Are there some slags who would force people into taking that way out, just to get their money? We all know there are. So I'm glad I don't have to make that deci-sion on whether it's OK to put old people down or not. Me, I'd like the option if I ever got there. You should get your choice of drug to go out on as well. What's the problem if someone wants to go out on the drink or drug of their choice? It's not like you're with-holding it for their health.

The one thing I take from this is that she's surrounded by people who love her, who go to see her and support her, fetch any little thing she likes. You read about these people who have been dead five years and no one ever knows. It must be terrible to be so isolated, particularly when you're ill and in pain. This is why I say again, family is everything.

It would be great to have my nan indoors, for us to look after her, but she's beyond that now. My mum and my dad can't look after her so it has to be the home. It's difficult to see her in there but it's the best place for her. The people who look after her are proper stand-up citizens. They look after her like she is family. I will always be grateful to them for that.

I don't know how I would feel, if I ended up there, having never lived, never done anything out of the ordinary. This is why I feel that life is for living and that goes for everything, from bungee jumping to trying a frog's leg.

When it comes to the end, will I be a burden on my family? I hope to be in my nan's position, to have got enough respect and love in my life that looking after me is something they want to do, rather than feel they have to. Mind you, look at my habits. I ain't ever getting a telegram from the Queen, am I? That's my pension pot – fags, booze, fatty food. I'll slip off when I'm in my sixties and the family can piss whatever money's left up the wall.

What is a good death? Can you plan one? I hope I go out having settled all the conflicts that I want to settle. I don't want to go to my grave hating people, or being hated, for that matter. So there's that idea of forgiveness – asking for it and giving it – before I die.

I don't want to have hundreds of doctors poking me about neither. If I'm fucked, I'm fucked and I'll accept it. Better go that way than clinging on to a tiny chance of survival. Mind you, easy to say now, maybe I'll feel different come the time.

I hope I can look back on my life and say I did the best I could with what I've been given.

I don't know how you'd feel if you was losing your mind. Perhaps it's a gentle way to go – forgetting who you are, where you are, just drifting off to become another little bit of the universe. That's the ideal anyway.

It's easy to say you should be allowed a living will, to say, 'If I have Alzheimer's to whatever degree, whack me up with the old "Goodnight Rover" cocktail, like vets use.' But you're someone else when you're in that situation. Your brain has changed and you might be completely happy lying in bed getting fed and changed three times a day. Killing you might really be to spare the pain of your relatives, not you.

Seeing my nan in there stops me worrying about stuff like debt too. Why wait for something? You never know what's around the corner and I wouldn't like to die thinking, 'Well, that was a boring last couple of years but at least I won't leave my credit card company out of pocket.' I think you should grab all the experience you can while you can and worry about the detail later.

12

If I saw the twelve-year-old me hanging around outside my house I'd go out and threaten the slag with a stick to make sure he went nowhere near my car.

Am I middle class? The missus buys scented toilet paper so I walk round with my arse smelling of cinnamon. I think that makes me middle class . . .

This is something that troubles me because I'm proud of my background and where I grew up. I'd like to think of myself as working class but can I really?

But, I can't deny that life has changed for me. I've sat down to dinner with Harold fucking Pinter, for fuck's sake. I've been hanging around with middle-class people for a lot of my life.

At first I found it uncomfortable – I was a bit of an object of fascination to people in the acting world. They had no respect for me – it was like, 'Surely this kid can't act. He's not gone to drama school, he's got no manners, he smokes, he speaks his mind.'

The whole thing about sitting around a table talking about the role was something I just couldn't do. I could do it now, though, easily. So I've changed.

One thing that does my nut in is when you hear these actors or writers banging on about their working-class roots and making out they're still the same people they were when they was back in the flats.

I'm certainly not, I'm really different. If I saw the twelve-year-old me hanging around outside my house I'd go out and threaten the slag with a stick to make sure he went nowhere near my car.

If you'd have told me back then that I'd be writing a book I would have told you to do one. The idea of writing my homework seemed mad enough.

I've met lots of different people and been exposed to a lot of ideas. Pinter was big for that with me but also the whole rave thing. It was a melting pot of back-grounds and you ended up having long conversations with people you'd never normally mix with. It was a leveller and an education. People are sometimes surprised I have thought about stuff as much as I have but that's largely due to years of head-melting conver-sations at chill-out clubs and parties.

Rave was my university, really. It was exactly like university, from what I can see, only with cleaner toilets and longer hours.

Only recently have I had a decent wedge I can rely on. I think people are surprised when they see my house. They think I live in a mansion but I live in an ordinary street with working people. It's three bedrooms, nice but no Premiership star's gaffe. This ain't some pose or out of a wish to stay grounded or any of that bollocks, it's all I could afford up until now.

If I had a choice, I'd stay working class. Still, when we didn't have so much cash, we made a few sacrifices and sent the kids to private school. That will make them middle class, won't it? So I'm choosing something for my kids I wouldn't choose for myself.

Sunnie talks incredibly posh. She puts a T in 'water', like 'waTer'. I hadn't heard anyone do that outside of a teacher before I was fourteen. She learns Mandarin. Mandarin! Sometimes I have to go and have a lie down when I think about it. I just can't believe a kid of mine is doing something as amazing as that.

Our kids really have reflected where I'm at in my career. Dani was born in Newham General, two leaflets on breastfeeding and thrown out the next day. Dani gets to a good age, six or seven, everything's on an even keel and Jo gets pregnant with Sunnie. This time we've got a bit of money so Sunnie was born in The Portland, a pukka maternity hospital in London. She don't know anything about Custom House, just goes back to see her nan now and again. To her, it's just a weird area. Sunnie gets to an easier age, six, and then Jo gets pregnant again. Arty comes along and he's born in Harlow because I don't quite have the money for The Portland no more. I've got three of the terrors now and I'm happy with that.

Some things have been puzzling to me. For instance, where I come from everyone uses the word 'cunt' all the time. Everyone, my mum, my nan, my dad, everyone. It's not seen as particularly offensive, it's just how people in the East End talk.

The people at school doing the bullying are the ones banged up now – for drugs, mainly. They were the cool kids, who always had the best trainers and best outfits but no education. I don't want that destiny for my kids.

But when I started acting I noticed that it made some people uncomfortable. I still only have a bit of an inkling why but I've learned to cut it out of my conversation around certain people.

Does that make me middle class? What do middle-class people say instead of 'the C word'? Given the melts you meet on a daily basis, it's a very handy word to have around.

Harold Pinter used to say the C word quite a lot. I suppose you can if you've got a Nobel prize on your mantelpiece.

So what is class? If it's down to your income or where you live, then I'm middle class. My daughter rides a horse. That's middle class, ain't it?

I saw this thing saying 'how to know if you're a success'. It included things like having a nanny – which to me would mean my fiancée wasn't as close to my kids, so that would be a token of failure. It was a checklist, almost like a Panini sticker album of middle-class life. It had things like: having a cleaner (got), annual skiing holidays (ain't got), fridge with ice dispenser (got), 400-thread sheets (wot?), a sit-on mower (not much good in my little back yard), a wine cellar (I've got a lager fridge instead). I ticked a fair few off on the list but, to me, none of this stuff shows you're a success. Being a success means getting up every morning and looking forward to the day ahead. That's it. If you're at a point in your life where you want to do what you do, then you're a success and it don't matter if you've got a seventy-inch plasma screen indoors or have to watch TV through a shop window.

I suppose in terms of stuff owned and lifestyle I shade it into the middle class. I still feel more comfortable around normal people than posh sorts, though.

And I still talk the same, I don't go much on watching theatre or opera or none of that shit. It's puzzling.

I suppose at the end of the day it don't matter to many people but it matters to me. I think it's important that I stay in touch with my roots. This is why I don't go for the celeb thing of only eating in posh restaurants or sticking to celebrity haunts. I want to be myself, just normal.

That gets harder and harder because of the mad life I lead.

The other thing is, of course, that my kids will be middle class. Will I still be able to talk to them or relate to them? I think I will but I might be in the same position with them as my old man was with me – knowing nothing about the life they're going into.

I hope little Arty is going to love football, I would really like that if he did. I don't know what he's going to do. I do know he's going to be a bit of a posh kid. Where does my influence come in there? Where is the cut-off point between how I was brought up and how he will be? I mean he's got me and Joanne at home, we still got the East London morals, we're as Cockney as each other, we swear a lot. But the kids take their cue from their social surroundings, that's what they learn from. Who knows what goes on when they leave the house? In the East End I had to worry about gangs and drugs. In Essex I have to worry about them falling off a horse and drugs. It's different, for sure.

But that's the other thing, kids don't play out like they did. There was something quite beautiful about the old East London, playing football down the street, playing wall ball, riding around on your bike, putting a bit of cardboard in the back wheel to make it sound like a motorbike. The idea of going out and being free and doing what you want is gone now. Arty will live a life with me running him around in the motor – which is so different to the way me and my dad were brought up. How will that affect him?

I have a lot of conflicting emotions. Like I want my kids to do well at school but I don't want it to drive us apart. When I was growing up it wasn't cool to study. You'd have been bringing a whole heap of pressure on yourself, bullying, everything, if you tried hard and got on with the teachers.

Mind you, the people at school doing the bullying are the ones banged up now – for drugs, mainly. They were the cool kids, who always had the best trainers and best outfits but no education. I don't want that destiny for my kids. Maybe it's just fear of the unknown that rattles me a bit.

So I'd like something different for my kids to what I had, but I admit I'm a bit scared of it. What if Arty or Sunnie want to be a lawyer or something? I wouldn't know how to advise them.

At the end of the day, people are people. It's just that it's very important for me to be close to my kids and I don't want anything to get in the way.

13

You need a thick skin as an actor, for sure, which is a pity because plenty haven't got one. The advice I've given to my daughter – who is setting off as an actor – is that for every one job you get, you lose out on twenty.

Acting is my passion, it's my life. Everything I am, I owe to it. I took to it from the first day I tried it in drama class, was always good at it. It always made me feel alive.

That said, I never planned anything. For me, it was just a hobby. If I could have seen where I am today when I was just beginning, I don't think I'd have had any way of understanding how it all happened.

I'm trying to bring a new style of acting to the soap world, and that could have gone either way. Thankfully people have embraced it and they're loving it. I watched some of my stuff on that show and I think it's some of the best work I've ever done. Without the swearing and with the restriction of it being a family audience it's a difficult platform for someone like me, it really is. But I think the limitations have made me, forced me to show new sides of my character.

I think no one can touch *EastEnders* at the moment, we took it to another level, all of us. We've got one of the strongest casts around, even going over the years. I know I would say this, but I think out of *Corrie*, *EastEnders* and *Emmerdale*, *EastEnders* is the best. At the moment. It changes all the time. *Hollyoaks* is full of beautiful people and good to look at. I love *Hollyoaks* – I said I'd never do it but ended up there for a bit and saw a different side of it. I've got a soft spot for them. I've become part of this soap club now.

For me, acting's about accessing different parts of yourself and portraying them honestly. I don't think you have to be 'man of a thousand faces' to be a good actor. You need to show your individuality, not disappear into a role.

I don't understand, when you go to RADA or another drama school, how sitting in a classroom with thirty other people gives you any individuality about your own technique. You come from all walks of life but you're told to become a blank canvas, throw away what you know.

I disagree. I think the greatest actors over time play themselves, or the most interesting part of themselves. We play with words, that's all it is, we take words and make them fascinating.

You can do a million accents but have a monotone voice and no one will want to listen to you. Look at all the American actors, Clint Eastwood, Christopher Walken, Tom Cruise. Tom Cruise did *Far and Away*, no one wanted to see it. Don't do an Irish accent, for god's sake, Tom. Do what you do. You're a movie star, you've got presence, you hold the screen.

These greats put on a suit and different pair of glasses and it's a different role. They're themselves but they're still completely convincing.

I love Christopher Walken. He has a rhythm and a music to the way he speaks, which belongs only to him. No one else can do that without immediately falling under his shadow.

I think, just from a career point of view, it's better to stick to your strengths. When you're an actor you're only ever one film or TV programme away from becoming famous, a success, and when you've done it, people want to see it again.

Method acting is not for me. This is when you stay in the role 24/7. If you're playing a pirate, presumably you hop about on a wooden leg all the time. I don't know, maybe you jump on a boat on the river and start waving your cutlass at passing boats.

Half the roles I've played, I'd have ended up inside if I method acted them. I mean, how do you method act a serial killer? Sixteen murders followed by forty years in Broadmoor is a bit over the top when it comes to preparing for a role. I'd rather just put a scary expression on me boat.

You've got your Daniel Day-Lewis, takes a year out to study a role. A year? To play Abraham Lincoln? All he did was put a top hat on.

He was in *My Left Foot* and was brilliant. But he wasn't really in a wheelchair. Someone was feeding him. I think 'wow', that's taking it to the extreme. He's won four Oscars, this geezer. He's got Oscar written all over him because it's all arty.

How do you become Abraham Lincoln, go back to the eighteenth or nineteenth century? How do you mix with Victorians? I like to do a bit of research now I'm older but to live and breathe it every day? For one, it's wanky. For two, it's too much hard work. When do you switch off?

And how do you get away with it indoors? If I came home playing someone who had lost their legs or something, can I ask my missus to push me about in a wheelchair? She'd cut my legs off if I did that, that would be the worrying thing.

It's horses for courses. I suppose you can do all that if you got no responsibilities, no children or anything like that. There's a lot of English actors who just drop everything and go to America, and they speak American the whole time they're there. I just act. I come in as me, act, turn back into me and get back in the haddock and go home. Of course you want to explore different avenues and different characters but you're still playing yourself essentially, still using what you've got to make every scene interesting.

You don't need to have lived as a character to summon up emotions.

Most of the time as an actor, you go with the scene. A well-written 'angry' scene will make you angry, because there is a point to it. It's how you get angry, because it's easy to shout and scream.

At the moment, the bosses let me change bits of my script, to add little bits. I get the point across but I do it slightly

How do you method act a serial killer? Sixteen murders followed by forty years in Broadmoor is a bit over the top when it comes to preparing for a role.

differently, slightly musically, I change words around just to make it sound a little bit more Mick.

If I'm going to be angry in a scene, I'm not going to level ten straight away, I'm going to build up to that and react to the other actor. I wait for their line, and if that line makes me angry, then I'll go. There's something about using your mince pies that shows you're angry without the need to shout.

You have to push yourself, be on it every day. What I try to do is to make every scene electric, so that the viewer wants to keep coming back to my storyline.

Too many soaps in the past had actors who were dead behind the eyes because they weren't pushing themselves and no one was pushing them. I won't let myself get away with that. I'm passionate about what I do and take pride in it.

Every scene in a film or a soap is a mini film, it has a beginning, a middle and an end. You have to find the beats in that scene. It doesn't matter if you do accents or whatever, or you high pitch your voice, it's just about keeping it interesting, end of. That's what we do.

There's still time for a few laughs. I sometimes have a half at the end of the day in The Queen Vic, though they started putting TCP in the pumps to stop me drinking it. That's a standard thing on soaps, like in the shops they inject the Mars bars and things with TCP to stop people nicking them.

It took me a while to find my voice as an actor. As a young actor you're getting pulled around, told you need to change your accent, be a chameleon. That wasn't what people wanted to see me do because I couldn't excel at it, I'm not very good at accents. I'd find that when I went for auditions with an accent, I'd be concentrating more on the accent than the actual acting. Okay I've nailed the accent but I've forgotten what I'm talking about. I'm worried about putting my tongue between my teeth for my THs, all this shit. I'm not going to go for all that. It's not a lack of ambition, I just can't be fucked.

I'm happy where I am and haven't got any immediate plans to do anything else.

It would take something really special to get me back into theatre again, especially since Harold's now dead. For me, theatre is a beautiful thing, it's a brilliant way of honing your craft, all that. It really gets my juices flowing for about three weeks and after that I start to find it really boring. To do a play for six months just completely stumps my brain. Unless a really cool play came up and it was just a four-week run, I don't think I'd want to do it. It's too demanding, you have to deliver the same thing every night and put your all into it so on the one side it's emotionally draining, on the other it's numbing and boring.

I think every actor, if you want to call yourself an actor, has to do that because it can define you and teach you stuff that you can't learn anywhere else, not in any drama school. I don't want to be a theatre star – that same journey to work, through rush-hour, getting there for quarter to six, going through the warm-up, all the talk about if it's going to be a full house, if there's a critic in, I get it but it's just not for me. I respect anyone who can do a twenty-year career in theatre but it is hard work. That idea of shitting your pants every night, which you do, particularly after you've fucked up, and I did fuck up. Until that happens, you have a little butterfly but you know what you're doing and it's fine.

Then you fuck up and it's all you can think about. You don't realize it can go wrong until then. I will never forget the feeling of it. I'd been an actor for about twelve years up to that point and always felt very confident. But it left me feeling weak and like I couldn't do it. Having that feeling in front of 1,000 people on Broadway was horrific. I think the bottom line is, I have never been a theatregoer. I'm not sure I can be bothered with the stress of going out to entertain all those upper-class people.

You need a thick skin as an actor, for sure, which is a pity because plenty haven't got one. The advice I've given to my daughter – who is setting off as an actor – is that for every one job you get, you lose out on twenty. She's a great little actress, she's done a couple of films. She doesn't ask for my advice on anything, maybe the odd line, how she can beef something up but not much. But in general I've told her, she has to do this on her own. She can't have me opening doors for her because, one, it's unfair on other people and two, she'll be exposed.

She's had a couple of knocks recently, and sits up in her bedroom, taking it badly. And it's a double-edged sword, because you need to get used to it, but really, you never want to get used to it. You don't want to get used to rejection, to walking in a room and thinking, 'I'm not going to get this.' They sniff that a mile off the producers and the directors and they don't give you the role, so it has to hurt you, when you miss out on a job so that it makes you so much more determined for the next audition.

When I was missing out on auditions, I always had faith in myself. I really felt that I was better than the majority of young actors out there. I'd lose out on parts to other people and I'd think, 'He couldn't lace my boots.' It would be a political thing rather than a talent thing. It was never that I was swimming in this acting world and felt like a tiny little fish, it was more like I was a big fish. The first job I ever did was with David Thewlis and Helen Mirren. I've stood up with David Jason, the cream of the British acting world, at a younger age, and never felt fear, so I knew that this was my calling. It was just convincing producers and directors of that.

I got pigeonholed by the press as a hard man and because of the way I speak and because I swore and perhaps because I have a bit of a swagger, but there's never been any reports of me fighting or anything like that. Don't get me wrong I would have loved to have done that a few times. I honestly don't know where they get this idea from, other than a few roles I've played. Even in *The Football Factory*, I'm a hooligan but I'm doubting it. I don't really want to be a hooligan, I've got wrapped up in this weird world, I sort of speak for the audience in a way and that's a tough thing to do. I have to touch millions of people who might be watching it and they're seeing the story through my eyes. You can't do that if you're just a straightforward thug.

When fame arrives, you need to be ready for it. I couldn't have done *EastEnders* at twenty, I don't know how these young kids get through it. I've had to draw on all my experience to do it, sometimes forty pages of dialogue a day. That's a film's worth in a week.

I do feel for some of these young kids. They're in a soap, the episode airs, they go to sleep that night and wake up famous. I wouldn't have been able to handle that, I would have gone right off the rails. I wouldn't have had the experience to do the discipline thing, I would have gone out every night, milking the fame thing because that's what you do when you are young. It's intoxicating. You think, 'I've made it, I'm famous, they love my character,' but you forget about the work. Thank God, everyone in *EastEnders* nowadays is very professional. All the young actors get a load of support from the show to help them adjust to life in the spotlight, and the feeling on set is calm, low-key and business-like – the way it should be.

The idea of joining *EastEnders* and of Mick Carter was to create the most perfect soap character. I thought, if we're going to go into this I want to create a soap character who can potentially be the best ever. He should have every attribute, alpha male, a touch of my feminine side, love the kids, love the missus, very protective of them. I've got funny lines, I've got Cockney slang which makes me different from every-body else. But at the same time, Mick's been in care as a kid and people feel sorry for him because he's been shunted around care homes all his life. It's the closest I've ever played to myself other than the care home thing. What we did was a characterization, so I sat down and they asked me loads of questions about my home life. It is a sort of mirror of my own life with my own missus. We've been together for years, had a kid young, never married – well, not for years.

So am I acting? Of course I am. I'm engaging my imagination, drawing on everything I've learned and known, trying every day to smash it. But when I get home I leave Mick at the door and become me again.

14

One thing's for certain, when it comes to discussing drugs, common sense flies out the window.

There ain't half some bollocks talked about drugs.

On the one hand you've got people making out that anyone who has a crafty spliff watching *Time Team* immediately goes mad and gets addicted to heroin.

On the other you've got the odd idiot pretending that filling yourself up with skag and living in a squat with a dead rat on a string for air freshener's in some way glamorous.

I'm a dad. I fear for my kids. This sort of thing really concerns me, but I think everything is heading in very much the wrong direction. We should be offering our kids protection. Instead we're exposing them to huge dangers. Let me run you through my thinking.

We're meant to be in a war on drugs, ain't we? Well, from where I'm standing it looks like the drugs won. Carrying on the war against drugs is like us carrying on the war against the Normans. We lost a long time ago. Live with it. Cocaine, it seems to me, is easier to get than a part for your boiler in this country.

When they're detecting cocaine in tap water because of the number of people taking it, I'd say it was time for a different approach. Don't get me wrong, I think cocaine is dangerous. It killed 200-odd people in the UK last year. You can't dismiss that. It's a powerful addictive drug which has the potential to fuck you up.

I tell you this, though, compared to booze and fags, it hasn't killed as many people. You look at the numbers of people dying from cigarettes – thousands and thousands a year – or the amount of people killed in one way or another by booze.

Banning drugs hasn't worked, ain't it about time to try something different?

But no, what we get is more of the same. Now comes the legal highs ban. This is funny more than anything. The government is like the aggressive little bloke in a pub fight who's already taken a schooling from about six others but decides to pick on the pub dog just to see if he can come out on top against someone. And then, inevitably, gets his bollocks ripped off.

Drugs were legal for most of history and the sky didn't cave in. Queen Victoria is believed to have taken cocaine with a young Winston Churchill – it didn't seem to affect their contribution to society. Going further back, even the cavemen chomped a bunch of mushrooms, sat painting mammoths on the walls and saying, 'What's it all about, then?'

People will get off their nuts on one thing or another. You will never stop that. You may as well try to ban people from having a Sherman tank.

Personally, if I'm coming home of an evening, I'd rather encounter a group of blokes who had been taking E than the same bunch who had been on the piss. From the drinkers you risk getting your head kicked in. The worst you'll get from the trippers is a bit of a sweaty hug.

The old Apple geezer Steve Jobs said LSD gave him the right outlook to be successful – concentrating on making great things rather than making money. But it's clear that the government don't want you to take that. They'd prefer you to take much more harmful stuff that dulls your brain rather than firing it up.

All 'psychoactive substances' should be illegal, they say. That means things that affect your nut. Well that's David Cameron done for then, because he does my head in. Seriously, what's a psychoactive substance? Glue? Aerosols? Petrol? Nutmeg? People use all these things to get out of it. Are you going to do the garage if they sell someone petrol they sniff? Of course not.

All right, how about a shop who sells you something they say is bath salts but you know lights you up like Oxford Street? Or, if a garden centre can sell a plant that gets you high, why can't a head shop? Have these muppets given all this a second thought? I've got one GCSE in drama and I can see it won't work, so if I was them I'd be asking Eton for the money back.

All over the world they've shown banning drugs causes more problems than it solves. It gives money to organized crime, puts people in danger when they take adulterated rubbish and leads those who might live a productive life into a spiral of debt and crime.

I doubt that Boots, were they allowed to stock narcotics, would put an iron door on the front, dial up the volume on the decks and terrorize the area until the swat team came in through the wall.

I know this because I grew up around it. There's fellas I knew who are now doing serious time in prison for drugs. They were bright blokes but the easy money tempted them – that and the total lack of education and opportunities caused by successive governments treating them like shite.

If you think that's a sob story, consider this – David Cameron got done for drugs at school and smoked them at university. He's been accused of that and never denied it, at least. Some of his mates got thrown out of Eton for drug-dealing. You can bet they aren't doing a twelve at the Scrubs now. Why? Because they had somewhere to go to get out of selling drugs. A lot of people I grew up with didn't.

I know people who finished up dead – through other criminals, through overdoses, all sorts. I've seen neighbourhoods wrecked by drugs. But it's not so much the drugs that caused this – it's the fact they're illegal.

How do I reckon that? Well, for starters, if drugs weren't illegal then when manufacturers fell out, they'd send round the solicitors, not Big Mike with a claw hammer in the back pocket of his G Stars. Also, I doubt that Boots, were they allowed to stock narcotics, would put an iron door on the front, dial up the volume on the decks and terrorize the area until the swat team came in through the wall.

For seconds, people would know what they're taking. You look at it this way – say someone gets seriously pissed and finishes up in A&E. The doctor asks what's up with them. Ten Jager Bombs and half a bath of lager. The doctor knows how to treat that. I don't know much about medicine, which may surprise those of you who saw me in *Casualty*, but I do know that finding out what someone's swallowed is half way to knowing what to do about it.

If the same geezer comes in next week flat on his back and the doctor asks, 'What's up with him?' his mates might reply, 'He took some pills he got from Wonky George round the back of Costcutter.' 'What were they?' 'Don't know.' The doctor, and I believe this is the medical term, is shafted. He don't know what was in them pills. And while he's finding out, someone could be dying.

So it seems to me the blindingly obvious thing to do about drugs is to license them, tax them, and offer some sort of quality control like we do with alcohol and cigarettes. Two hundred billion a year worldwide goes on drugs. Next to arms and oil, it's the world's biggest market. But you and me don't get a sniff of the tax money. Imagine what could be done with that. Imagine the positive changes that could be made, not just to our lives but to those of the miserable sods caught up in drug production – all them kids in Mexico dying, snared in the drug war. In fact, there's so much money in it, it makes you wonder if someone's taking backhanders from the drug dealers to keep drugs illegal. They love it that way.

You see, I just don't get it. I can sit here puffing on a cigarette – and I do – despite the fact it's 100 per cent proven to be bad for me. However, if I want to take ecstasy – which I don't – then I can't. People have died on it? Yes, but many more people die on aspirin and we don't ban that. We control it, issue information leaflets with it.

Most of the deaths that have occurred seem to be down to bad batches anyway. If someone dies of food poisoning, we don't say, 'Sorry, squire, a moody chicken killed him. That's chicken banned, then.' We sue the chicken seller and crack on.

People should be able to know what they're buying – not get stuff made by some greasy hippy in a kitchen laboratory who chucks in half the cleaning products if he's in the mood. OK, you might say, 'People taking this stuff know the risks.' But loads of these risks are created by the laws against drugs.

This, in the end, is what does my nut in – people seem incapable of seeing reason on this subject, or even of using reason.

If the government's own adviser says something's largely harmless – as they have with lots of illegal drugs – then shouldn't the government follow his advice? But what do they do? They sack the poor melt for producing an honest report that they asked for and then ban a load of other stuff they have no evidence about at all.

Yet booze and fags are fine because they have lobby groups and money behind them. The little bloke selling magic mushrooms at a market isn't going to give an MP a £100,000 pay cheque as a non-executive director to turn up two afternoons a month, sexually harass the receptionists and drive off in his Bentley again. It just shows that, for all they go on about looking after the small guy, they are full of pony.

It is a diabolical liberty. What right has David Cameron got to tell you what to do just because he thinks that if he lets you take something harmless, someone in Surrey won't vote for him? Dave, relax. Surrey's off its swede now and again like the rest of the country, they'll love ya for it, ya mug.

The politicians will say stuff like, 'We're not convinced these things are harmless.' Well, you being convinced is nothing to do with it, sunshine. You have to produce evidence. And if 'being convinced' is something to do with it, how much more evidence do you want against cigarettes? No, hang on, don't ban them as well, I like a fag. Note to kids – not big or clever to smoke. I wish I'd never started.

The thing is, though, Dave don't think you're capable of making your own decisions. You can be thirty-five years old, enjoying a spliff with your mates in the privacy of your own home, causing harm to no one and he thinks he has the right to break in your front door and cart you away. But if you drink yourself to death on two bottles of whisky a night while kicking the kids and beating the wife and that's nobody's business but your own. In fact, his mates who own the supermarkets will help you do it with cheap deals on booze.

I know some people will think I've got an axe to grind here and it's true that I had my moments when I was younger. But I've seen the damage that illegal drugs can do, seen the problems caused by turning their manufacture and sale over to some of the nutters I grew up around.

I'm a dad, a family man. I want my kids to be protected. They sure aren't now with the present laws and it looks like those in power are set on making things worse, not better.

15

Why can't people concentrate on the positive, rather than filling themselves up with spite?

I don't think the human race is ready for Twitter. We're not evolved enough to treat each other kindly and well on it. It has the potential for being a great thing, increasing understanding around the world, allowing you to see little glimpses into the lives of people totally unlike you.

Instead, it's simply used by someone you've never met to tell you you're a melt and he hopes you die.

You read stuff about yourself on Twitter that you can't believe. I had to do Twitter because I had about ten different parodies, some of them with 15,000 followers. Geezer Danny, all that. I thought the only way to stop this is to do it myself. I realize that I've got quite a weird warped brain which enjoys a bit of to and fro – so I do like it in some ways. I think the idea of Twitter for me is that if you're going to tweet, tweet something. Don't say you're crossing the road or eating ya dinner. Have something about ya.

I don't think we humans are quite ready to express ourselves on Twitter. All it seems to do is breed hatred and bitterness. This is a generation of people who were bullied as kids who now have a voice and can hide behind screens.

Some of the stuff I've had said to me is horrendous. I was trending once, which means a lot of people are talking about you. Some people were saying, 'Please tell me it's because he's dead.' And they really did mean it, genuinely, they were praying and hoping that I'd gone quietly in the night. That would have made them really happy.

They was so disappointed I wasn't dead. Yet they know nothing about me, they never met me.

This was in the period I was going through when I couldn't catch a cold. I couldn't get no work. I was down to doing personal appearances, poxy clubs, standing behind a rope and brassing my arse off, sticking my arse in the air and saying, 'Fuck me, I'm a celebrity.'

Actually, I wouldn't be surprised if 'Fuck me, I'm a Celebrity' becomes a reality show. The way I was going at that point, I'd have ended up on it. That'd make your bushtucker challenge look a bit more appetizing, wouldn't it?

Let's be fair, I'd begun to be viewed as a bit of a liability. I'm stuck in the old-school mould of Oliver Reed. I like to drink and I'm never afraid to talk about that, never afraid to give a comment and call it like I see it.

This is when people could laugh at me. I'd fight back on Twitter, mostly I'd pull their pants down and ruin 'em. Now that's stopped but it still goes on for other people.

Leigh Francis, the comic who plays Keith Lemon, has said Twitter trolls have made him scared to go out. He says he gets grief every day and has had people – who, remember, have never met the geezer – saying they wish he'd die of AIDS. It's left him scared to go clubbing in case he gets clumped by some jealous melt.

Half the time we know that these tweets are done by fifteen-year-old boys in some bedroom in Nantwich or somewhere who are just impressing themselves by being nasty in between visits to porn sites.

The trolls don't even have to get the right person to have a go. PR woman Sarah Moyes has nothing at all to do with the old Man U manager David Moyes but she got mistaken for his daughter. The abuse she got was disgusting. Lots of threats of rape, that sort of thing. I can only assume these trolls use the threat of rape so much because they're frustrated little arseholes who never get any sex.

There is no limit to how low they will go, protected by the anonymity of a keyboard. Claudia Winkleman's little girl's dress caught fire and the trolls laid into her, making sick jokes. What about these people who attack Madeleine McCann's parents? Them who had a go at Tom Daley when he missed out on a medal, telling him his dead dad would be ashamed of his performance? What kind of worm does that? Where is your life at that you get your kicks that way?

If you've got a bit of spite in you that needs getting out, go and kick off at West Ham or Millwall or Leeds. I can think of any number of firms who'd gladly fight you if you fancy it. You want a ruck, have it with someone who can fight back.

Some of the trolls, when they get caught, reveal that they aren't exactly the sharpest tools in the shed. One bloke in court said he had treated rape threats as 'a compliment'. He'd had a go at a couple of women who were trying to get the writer Jane Austen on a bank note. I've got a question for him: 'Why not use the time you spent doing that to spread some love in the world? Why not just be nice?'

His defence was hilarious. I ain't exactly Kavanagh QC but I tell you this, the defence 'My threat to brutally assault you was my way of saying you are beautiful,' ain't gonna cut it in any court I've heard of.

Chuck yer hands up and say 'guilty' mate, you'll get off lighter.

Half the time we know that these tweets are done by fifteen-year-old boys in some bedroom in Nantwich or somewhere who are just impressing themselves by being nasty in between visits to porn sites.

But some older people do them too. I would love a psychologist to explain it to me. Or maybe I don't need one. Maybe it's just poxy little rats with shit lives trying to make themselves feel better by making other people feel worse.

For every hundred tweets of love I get one that is a bit tricky but before it would be fifty–fifty. I was aware I could be easily mocked – why not? Cocky, gobby star, down on his luck, let's all queue up to take a swipe at him.

But now going on to *EastEnders* is giving me this thing where I can show people that I'm an actor and the people on Twitter are responding to that. There's so many people out there who didn't know I was an actor. I don't know how it was so much of a surprise, it's how I've been plying my trade for twenty-five years. Yes, I've done documentaries and stuff and I've become a bit of a personality, been on *Eight out of Ten Cats* and *Celebrity Juice* and all that, and I suppose that got in the way of people seeing my work clearly.

Now I can show people what I can do on a massive platform and take it to the next level.

People have much more contact with actors, musicians and others in the public eye than they ever did. That is great and I genuinely love talking to fans and even to others who ain't fans. Twitter can be a beautiful thing – it allows you to stay in contact with people you might lose otherwise. But I do fail to understand why someone would take time out of their day just to have a pop at a geezer they've never met. For me, life's too short.

When you're having a laugh with someone or there's a big event on and you can share it with everyone, that's brilliant. During treacle World Cup, I loved cheering on the team through Twitter, having people come back to me, all that.

But I suppose in the end it comes back to what I've said throughout this – why can't people concentrate on the positive, rather than filling themselves up with spite? I don't know the answer. Perhaps someone on Twitter can let me know.

16

There's no underlying talent they're trying to express. They're like a mirage produced by the heat of public interest. When that heat goes, there's nothing left.

I'm in two minds about reality TV because there is something quite honest about it. On *The Only Way is Essex*, when they cry they are crying properly, really feeling it. They're not actors, otherwise they're the greatest actors in the world. So I like that – it's refreshing and something different to what normal dramas and soaps offer you.

There's a downside, though, and I feel sorry for the kids who are on it.

They allow producers to manipulate them because they want more fame and more airtime. That disgusts me and it puzzles me. Why do they do it?

It's not about money, I think they only get paid about £50 a day but they just want fame and quickly. All right, they may get to sleep with a few people off the back of it, do the odd personal appearance but, to me, it's demeaning. And for most of them it leads nowhere.

I know agents that have had people call them up and say, 'I want a career as an actor,' and they say, 'What have you been in?' and they say, 'Big Brother number whatever.' They expect that's going to be their ticket to fame but they're sadly mistaken.

It's the equivalent of having a kick about with your kids in the back yard and then phoning up a professional club, telling them they should sign you because you put three past your six year old.

I wonder how many of them go into it with their eyes open. Once they've got the fame, they then want respect but they're never going to have the respect. People will recognize them in the street and want their photograph with them and all that but they forget that there's no mileage in what they're doing. They don't actually *do* anything.

While the show's airing they can do personal appearances and things like that, some of them open shops. All right, it's a little ride. But they never ever will have respect from their peers within the showbusiness world. They will always be the lowest in the pecking order unless they're at some nightclub in Kidderminster, where they'll be the highest. But at the National TV Awards or the BAFTAs or things like that, then they are low down.

I don't understand some things about these people's popularity. You look at Liev Schreiber, a brilliant actor from Hollywood. He gets 80,000 followers on Twitter.

What does that say about the world, when he gets 80,000, a brilliant actor like that, and some people who are famous just for being mean-minded melts have half a million followers? I mean, life isn't all about Twitter followers but it is a reflection of people's interest in you. You've got Cameron Diaz with half a million followers and Mark Wright with 2.7 million.

Weirdly, these people seem to court exactly the type of attention I'd prefer to avoid. They love being in the public eye because it's all that sustains them. There's no underlying talent they're trying to express. They're like a mirage produced by the heat of public interest. When that heat goes, there's nothing left.

Those who do get out of reality TV with a career normally have to demean themselves, turn themselves into caricatures. Take *Sun* columnist Katie Hopkins. All she'd done in the public eye was *The Apprentice*. Now she spews out hate for a living. She thinks she's saying what everybody else is thinking. Bollocks. I've never

People will recognize reality 'stars' in the street and want their photograph with them and all that but they forget that there's no mileage in what they're doing. They don't actually do anything.

seen one human being alienate so many people. Women, men, gay people, immigrants, everyone she's attacked. She seems to delight in being nasty. Who's she going to have a go at next, puppy dogs and kittens? She attacked me about my missus proposing to me yet has strong views on feminism. I just don't get it. There is no hatred of the bird. I think she just thought I was some thick idiot from East London and I had no wit or articulation. She's decided that being notorious is the way to go for her. But to me, it would be better to go back to a normal job, or even go on the dole. At least you would have your dignity.

17

You ask yourself, who's more attractive to women – Peter Andre or Marlon Brando? One's never out the gym, the other was never out the fridge. Let that be a lesson to us all.

I saw a slogan on a poster showing a ripped-looking bloke once – 'It never ends' – meaning the quest for improving your body always goes on. To me, it never begins.

Human beings come in all shapes and sizes and it's possible to be attractive as most of 'em. All right, if the fire brigade are having to hoist you out of your bedroom window then you might want to lose the pizza delivery firm's number but, really, most of us are fine as we are.

Trying to force yourself to live up to some idea of what your body should look like is more a sign you need to look at your priorities rather than your gut. It's a funny, paranoid, childish way to go on. Better get comfortable round yourself and think about the stuff that really matters, I'd say.

Also, is being attractive the be all and end all? Is it

the only measure of your worth? Mother Theresa was hardly a looker, was she? Did Oskar Schindler say, 'I know I saved all them people, but look at me. Bald! I'll always feel like shit.'

Women obviously have more pressure on them to conform to a beauty stereotype than men. I don't see why they should bother, though. I've said before, Jo is my perfect woman. I love her however she looks. But, if I'm gonna be honest, I prefer Jo's body after she's had a baby, when she's got a bit of weight on her. She doesn't believe me but it's true, I do. She's softer, more cuddly. I much prefer a woman who's got a bit of a Derby on her to one of these birds who've got a six pack. Not my thing at all. I have always preferred people who looked a bit unconventional – I don't like the artificial look, fake tan, fake tits, fake nails. I much prefer someone who looks unusual, a bit awkward or someone who really stands out. In my mind it's better to be 7ft tall in glasses than a 5' 8" glamour model.

There's this culture of perfection nowadays but it's people's imperfections that make them interesting.

The women I used to fancy most when growing up were Madonna and Victoria Wood, the comedian – and everyone in between. I thought Victoria was a classy bird, proper talented and funny and a great musician. There's something very sexy about her and I got quite jealous of her husband, who was a magician.

It prejudiced me against magicians for a bit, the rabbit-smuggling slags.

But that's what's truly attractive, isn't it? A zest for life, a bit of personality. No matter what someone looks like, you ain't gonna find them sexy if they've got the personality of a plank.

There's too much emphasis on women being thin by far. Size zero and all that is about women showing off to other women, men don't find that attractive at all. I am a heterosexual man. I like women who look like women, not boys. The Hollywood look don't really do it for me. Does a bloke want to get into bed next to someone who's all angles and ribs? May as well buy a greyhound and get that to cuddle up to you at night. You don't want to put your arm around a bird who looks like she could be in trap one in race three at Romford.

Of course, there's a whole industry devoted to making you miserable about your body, both men and women. You have this thing when celebs give birth: 'Amazing, she lost the baby bulge in three weeks.' Well, don't bother, love, because you looked better with it. That weight's there for a reason. If it's meant to come off, it'll come off and, if it don't, so what? If your old man can't see past a bit of flab then you're best ditching him and getting a proper bloke.

I see them men's fitness magazines and it's like the language of aliens to me. 'Get a six pack!' You ask yourself, who's more attractive to women – Peter Andre or Marlon Brando? One's never out the gym, the other was never out the fridge. Let that be a lesson to us all.

You might have a beautiful body but it gives you an ugly mind, paranoid, obsessive, boring, not that I'm saying Peter Andre is any of those things. Let's face it, we all look shit eventually. Better do it now so you have time to get used to it.

Most of this stuff about people needing to buff up comes from magazines that are trying to sell you things. Women have suffered this for years but now they're coming for the blokes. They tell you all men today are under the microscope. You need to be fit, you need a skincare routine, you need nutritional balance. I am no different, I admit.

Every Saturday night I follow the same skincare routine. I have discovered a wonderful infusion of rich grains, distilled water and yeast. It's called 'beer' and I take it internally. I find that after a few pints of this wonderful substance, my appearance and that of everyone else is greatly improved.

Then I light some Native American sacred herb, known as 'tobacco' and have a good puff on that. And for nutrition, I pack in the protein with a lamb korma. You have to have protein, I saw that on the cover of *Men's Health*, I believe.

My regime complete, I often take an essential beauty nap on the sofa until about four in the morning, at which point I will wake, remove toxins from my body by having a piss and climb into bed.

I do suck the life out of those aloe vera drinks, so that cancels out all the fags and fatty food anyway, don't it? I like that little battle. I wonder what goes on inside your body when you're sucking on a Benson and swigging aloe vera. Let them have an inner war. Bring it on.

There ain't nothing wrong with exercising to be fit, of course. But if you want to get fit, play football like a normal person. Being in a team will also stop you crawling too far up your own arse as the relentless piss-taking of your mates will keep your feet on the ground.

There's something very sexy about Victoria Wood and I got quite jealous of her husband, who was a magician. It prejudiced me against magicians for a bit, the rabbit-smuggling slags.

I'm not a kid any more and I think a man of a certain age should look like he's lived a bit. There's nothing wrong with a bit of a gut, it shows you're not some self-obsessed melt worried about what everyone else is thinking of them.

The other reason to go to a gym, of course, is to put on muscle to intimidate other blokes. But that means that you're a scared little rabbit inside. All right, for some criminals it's a tool of the trade, I accept that and there's an excuse for hitting the weights or even the 'roids. Not a very nice excuse, but an excuse. The rest of us should just chill out a bit.

Women aren't really drawn to muscle men anyway – they want someone who looks confident and chilled with themselves. Some gay men go for the roidy look, I know, but I can't really comment on that because I don't know anything about it.

All this 'product stuff' they try to sell young men is just that – a sales opportunity. My dad's gone his whole life without using moisturizer, having his eyebrows plucked or splashing himself in 'high-performance' shampoo. They've taken women for mugs for years and now they're trying to do the same thing to blokes.

It's just not what a proper bloke does. Do you think the big men of history spent a long time with grooming products? Did the Duke of Wellington say, 'I can't make Waterloo today, I simply can't do a thing with my hair'? Did Churchill go low fat? Did Bobby Moore check himself in the mirror before nicking the ball off Pelé? Of course not.

These were men the whole world looked up to. They wouldn't have been seen dead with cucumber on their eyes. Pampering – another load of old toss. OK, women like it but my idea of pampering happens at the spa known as The Dog and Duck.

I went on holiday last year and, typical Brit, got roasted alive on day one. I had to have this full body wrap. They lashed me up like a mummy. I stood it for about five minutes and then had to get out of it. I just don't feel comfortable like that. I suppose you could say it's insecurity. As a bloke, part of your identity is being able to look after yourself. Being treated like a baby just doesn't float my boat.

Plastic surgery is another 'no' for me. I wouldn't do Botox, I need my face, it is important. I need expressions. Also, just sitting there with some melt whacking needles in your head – no, not for me.

The only thing I would have done is my tits, which have arrived recently, my little man cups. What happened? Years ago men didn't have tits. Is it the processed food we eat nowadays? I don't mind having a couple of chins, I don't mind having a bit of an arse on me or having a bit of a belly. Do not give me a pair of tits, please. Anything but tits. Could I have them sucked out? Drained out? They irritate me. I know it's down to booze and eating shit and all that, but my dad's the same and he hasn't got tits. He's got gout in his leg, but no tits! Give me gout any day of the week but do not give me A-cup tits! I don't want 'em!

I've had to go to the gym sometimes because it's been my job to stay in shape for some films and all that. To be honest, I mugged it off pretty quickly. The

18

Nothing is more powerful than having heart and spirit. As long as you believe in yourself you don't have to be Ricky Hatton. Spirit will get you through.

I understand the obsession with violence and I do think it's something very much inbuilt in men. But there are ways that can be healthy and ways it can be unhealthy. Personally, I'd rather swerve it, if at all possible.

Sometimes it's not possible and you have to have it. Most of the time it can be avoided by just looking at the world with the right attitude – friendly, forgiving, and open to people.

I saw that film *A Bronx Tale* the other night with Robert De Niro. It's a beautiful little film about this kid growing up in the Bronx and a gangster who takes a shine to him. He loves him like his own son. The trouble is his own dad loves him too and he confronts this gangster over it, puts everything on the line because he loves him so much.

It's powerful, that is, because the dad's looking out for his son and he walks up to the gangster who is standing there with all his cronies and just confronts him and the gangster clumps him. He goes home and summons up the courage to confront him again. There's something about that that touches me, the fact that you would do anything for your family, even if you can't hold your hands up.

Violence comes naturally to some people. Not to me. I can hold my hands up and I will if I have to, but it's not deep in my bones.

As men we would all like to have that element we could dig into, that psyche if we need it now and again. To be able to stand there and clump three geezers who are taking the piss out of your missus, we'd all like to be able to dig into that.

Violence in this country has gone right off the boil compared to when I was growing up.

Eighty per cent of men will walk away from violence because they don't want trouble, they don't want that in their life. But if you get moved enough so you have no choice it's a primal thing that makes you stand up and be counted.

Sometimes you got no choice but to take the law into your own hands. Like I said going back to the whole East London thing, if you don't show any of that then you'll get walked all over. And your family will be walked over and you'll be known as a piece of crap. As long as you stand up, you'll be fine. Nothing is more powerful than having heart and spirit. As long as you believe in yourself you don't have to be Ricky Hatton. Spirit will get you through. It goes for everything – job interviews, relationships.

So that's all very well if you have no choice. But you don't want to overthink violence or start letting it dominate your life.

This is why I don't get the martial arts. Why do I want to spend three nights a week for ten years having some melt who thinks he's Japanese with magic powers shouting at me, telling me I need 'discipline'? So I can have it in a kebab shop if it comes on top? I'd rather hold my hands up, give it a go and take my battering if I have to. Then I pick up my large doner and chips and get on with my life.

And do martial arts really do all that good? People who attack you don't write you a letter to tell you they're about to kick off. The first thing you normally know about it is the paramedic asking you to focus on the light on the end of his pen.

You're also training yourself to be paranoid, running over scenarios of 'if this bloke comes at me this way, or if this other bloke tries to nut me'. You attract trouble. If you're known as a hard man, you can be sure there'll be a queue of people waiting to show you they're harder.

Look, I understand what motivates all this. All blokes want to think they're hard when they're young and I suppose it's natural to want to toughen up but you're either born that way or you ain't. Those of us who ain't are in the lucky position of being able to forget about all that and sit in watching Amanda Holden on autopilot at night instead of sweating our bollocks off in a church hall or boxing gym. Most of the hard men I've ever known have never been near a martial arts gym anyway.

It seems to me the best way of being a hard case is to have a dad who beats the granny out of you on a regular basis, start smoking when you're eight and get expelled from at least three schools for fighting. The trouble is, they don't do classes in that. To be clear, I'm not recommending anyone do that.

The best way of defending yourself is to be nice to people. That won't always work but, if it don't, all right, have it. If you can't have it, have it on your toes or do what you can. Don't worry about it.

Violence in this country's gone right off the boil anyway compared to when I was growing up. All right, some areas are still moody but mostly it feels much safer on the streets. You have to be unlucky to get involved in most places. Of course it happens, no one's saying it don't, but the days when you took your life in your hands going to a football match or a gig are long gone. I used to need eyes in the back of me swede with all the slags that was about when I was a teenager but now I find life very chilled. OK, that could be because I've moved out of Custom House and into Essex, which is relatively crime free, or at least random violent crime free.

The reason people think it's all coming on top is because the crime figures are recording almost anything as violence. I saw the other day a bloke had a biscuit thrown at him and that was recorded as a crime of violence. Another one was a kid being brushed with a nettle. It ain't exactly the Krays, is it?

This white-collar boxing thing makes me put my head in my hands too. There's a whole bunch of actors, writers, city boys and people like that who get into boxing because basically they think what they do isn't really a bloke's job.

They're right. Blokes' jobs are hard, dirty and difficult, so anyone in their right mind's gonna prefer a soft job. You give the average plasterer a chance to work in a job where he gets to sit on his arse all day getting paid five times the wages and he'll be off halfway through a skim finish.

So these white collar blokes get in the ring with some other soft sod, or some pro whose flattering them, and feel a bit better inside, less of a failure as a man. In a way I feel sorry for 'em because they're only responding to what society puts on 'em – and I suppose I'm a bit responsible. I've been in enough films that feature hard men, and Hollywood doesn't often portray the sensitive type as a hero.

However, can I suggest, if you're that attached to making yourself feel like a hard man, nick off up the Appleby Horse Fair and tell the gypsies that you can do the lot of them. More of a challenge than fighting some interior designer with an inferiority complex.

If you ain't got it, you ain't got it. You can train all you like.

Anyone I ever knew who became a boxer did it for money, one way or another. I've got big respect for them – it's the toughest job. But why the fuck would you want to risk having your brains dribble down your nose unless you had to? What are you proving? There's no point being the bravest man in East London Cemetery. If there's a point to it, then sweet. You might win money in the ring, you might use your boxing as a doorman or a gangster – fair play then – but who wants to put in all that sweat just to feel better about themselves?

Seeing my kids playing happily in the garden does that for me.

We need to chill a little bit, I'd say. *Sun on Sunday* and *GQ* columnist Tony Parsons makes me smile with this sort of thing – he's always going on about how people are getting weapons and leaving them by the side of their bed or giving instructions about what to do in a fight. My instruction for being in a fight is, if you need instructions about what to do in a fight, don't get in a fight.

Calm down, Tony, breathe in, mate, it ain't gonna happen to you. Don't tell people how to behave in a fight. You sound like Gareth off *The Office*. You live in Hampstead. Is someone going to assault you with Dead Sea Bath Salts and a Lavazza coffee scoop? I used to live in Hampstead for a bit when me and Jo split up, and believe me, mean streets it ain't. It's a nice place, friendly people, like a lot of London. They have the odd thing go on, same as anywhere, but no one's gonna crawl into your bedroom and knock you over the head with a bag of quinoa.

My instruction for being in a fight is, if you need instructions about what to do in a fight, don't get in a fight.

The gaffe I lived in in Hampstead, we used to leave the door open a lot of the time – that is because most of us was too fucked to remember to close it, admittedly, but we never had no trouble there.

I'd like to reach out to Tony, encourage him to get a bit of perspective on life, find love in his heart instead of fear. He seems to live in a world where at any minute you could be beaten to death for looking at someone wrong. There are places like that but, if I was him, I wouldn't worry that's going to happen while he's chomping on his sourdough roll on Hampstead Heath. What's he afraid of? Unsolicited advice on soft furnishings? I hear that on Hampstead High Street they had a drive-by shouting once.

I live in Essex, which is like South Central LA compared to Hampstead, but I don't feel threatened walking about. It's a peaceful area, which is why I chose it.

I must confess, though, I keep a hammer by my bed, just in case. It's a squeaky one I nicked off little Arty. I have this dream about clowns and I want to be able to defend myself, should one ever come leering through the mirror. Don't laugh, it could happen.

I've got nothing against Tony Parsons, by the way, other than him voting UKIP – not the London way, son, not the London way at all. He talks some sense, some bollocks too. Like the rest of us, really, except he's managed to work it so he gets paid for it. Crafty. On balance, though, I'd rather have a bit of Nicholas Parsons. He seems more comfortable in his skin.

There's so much more to being a man than being able to hold your hands up. A much bigger challenge is making your partner happy, looking after your kids right if you've got them. It's a bit weird that blokes will look up to some hard case but not to a single father or someone who steers his kids through a difficult patch. We face bigger challenges in this life than violence, that's for sure, but we don't seem to spend time obsessing about them. There's no training class to prepare you for losing someone you love, you can't tool up to keep your kids on the straight an' narra. Compared to that, facing some pissed-up twat who wants to clump you is easy. We shouldn't think about it so much. And if we spent time trying to be nicer, rather than convincing ourselves we're all rufty tufty, then maybe the world would improve for women too. For all men obsess about being able to hold their hands up, it's often women who have to live under the shadow of male violence, something I'm very aware of having daughters.

19

If you're working forty hours a week and you can't cover your bills, that ain't your fault.

Some people will tell you that if you're not a success, then it's your fault. Sometimes this will be true but most of us get where we are through a mix of talent, hard work and luck. You can do something about only one of those things, really.

A lot of successful people just happened to have been in the right place at the right time. There are plenty with no discernible talent whatsoever who have big jobs in showbiz, government, even plumbing, in my experience of the rob dogs I've dealt with sometimes.

People bang on about benefits culture, all that. There are piss-takers, no one doubts that. But I know plenty of people on benefits who work hard – it's just they don't get paid enough to cover the basics of life. Now you can say, 'Get off your arse and get a better job.' All right, say everyone does that. Whose gonna actually do the shitty jobs then?

If you're working forty hours a week and you can't cover your bills, that ain't your fault. It's the fault of the slags paying you. So if you have to claim benefits, claim 'em and don't feel bad about it. It's not you who's really getting the benefit anyway, it's your employer. They pay you shit all and expect the state to pick up the rest of the tab.

All right, it's good to be ambitious, but up to a point. If we're all ambitious, a lot of us are going to be disappointed. One thing we can learn from the older generation is to be happy with what we've got. It's like me. I do get managers, people like that, pushing me to go to Hollywood. At the end of the day, I can't be arsed. I'm on a good wedge here, doing a job I enjoy, so why bother?

It's about being happy with yourself. My dad's a painter and decorator. Now that was never for me. Frankly, I'd rather have been on the dole than getting up grafting for next to nothing. I did it for a bit but binned it.

I don't like the fact that people are made out to be lazy scroungers if they are claiming benefits. JK Rowling wrote the Harry Potter books on benefits and she's paid that back a fair bit. The entire eighties music industry came about because a load of people had the chance to spend time developing on the dole. It ain't the end of the world, nor shameful, to be claiming benefits. People take out now, maybe they put back later.

Also, when I was a kid you'd see these visions of the future where all the manual labour was done by machines and people would live in a leisure society.

What the fuck happened to that? The machines took the jobs but the other side of the bargain was fucking nowhere. If you're one of them people who for generations would have been happy stamping a hole in a bit of metal for forty years, then society allows the company to come up with something to replace you, shouldn't that society owe you and your class of people some compensation? You can't just say, 'Here, you, we've replaced you with a machine, it works ten times as hard and it don't fart or moan about the weather. Go and become an orchestra conductor or something machines can't do, will ya?'

The only people reaping the benefit of these machines are the company owners. So they've taken a fucking wrecking ball to society and, instead of being asked to front up and pay for that, they're allowed to walk away with the profits. In fact, they're seen as a good thing. While the poor slags who now don't have any work, and whose sons and daughters don't have any work are told they're fucking lazy. It's like self-driving trains. You can't stick them on the network and then complain that a whole load of people who would have been train drivers then go on the dole and don't immediately doff their cap and be grateful to go and work for minimum wage. They kick you in the nuts and expect you to open your legs again and say, 'Would you like another go?' We should say, 'Your job's been replaced. Part of the cost of replacing that job is to cover your wages until retirement. Off you go, son, 'ave it on the golf course for twenty-five years, good luck to ya!'

But the train companies, and a lot of companies like them, are only interested in cutting costs, not paying for the damage they cause to whole ways of life. We've got into a situation where people say that's progress! Not from where the train driver's sitting it ain't!

There are people who should never be allowed near any sort of job owing to their massive capacity to fuck it up.

This would hold back growth, stop us being internationally competitive if it was rolled out across all industries – that's what they'd have you believe. No it wouldn't, it would just stop a load of rich people getting richer at the expense of ordinary people. In fact, giving people proper compensation when they lost their jobs would put a massive cash injection into the economy. The newly unemployed would have to have something to fill their days and the leisure industry would go mental. Instead, no, let's just allow some billionaire to stick it in a tax haven where it does nothing.

Also, 'competitive'? What does that mean? Constantly rising standards of living? For who? Not the people laid off. We need to make sure them standards are going up for everyone and that might involve accepting that the unemployed have as much right to a nice life as anyone else.

The moralizing over this sort of shit kills me. We've got two million-odd unemployed, why should they all be people who are unhappy with being out of work? Surely if those who like to doss are allowed to get on with it, it frees up jobs for them who like them. I'm not saying it's right, but it's not like you're living in luxury on the dole. You get about £57 a week if you're living in a couple. If you can clothe and feed yourselves and pay your bills on that, if you're happy like that, why not? You free up a job for someone who wants to go and earn £300 or so as a decorator.

There's a big hypocrisy about work. You hear people saying about the unemployed: 'Some of 'em don't want to work.' Well, apart from the very few of us who are lucky enough to do something we enjoy, who does?

Are you telling me that everyone in this entire country wants to work? How many lottery winners keep their jobs? But if you admit you don't want to work and you actually act on that, you're seen as lazy. If you think working stacking shelves is hard, try living on £57 quid a week, with only Jeremy Kyle to fill your days. It's enough to drive you to work.

You hear experts saying unemployment is necessary to the country – it makes the whole system work. Why then, if someone has to be unemployed, are they expected to be unhappy about it? It's because the world we now live in wants to shame people into taking shit jobs for fuck-all pay. Increase the wages for the low paid and you'll see people coming off the dole and other benefits quick enough.

'You shouldn't be dependent on people,' they say. But the boss who makes money out of low-wage workers is dependent on them, the bankers are dependent on massive benefits, the power industry on huge subsidies. But that's OK because they wear suits, not hoodies and trainers.

It's OK to claim £500,000 on taxes if you're sitting knocking one out over reruns of *Peak Practice* in a minister's office. Claim a fraction of that doing the same from a sofa in Canning Town and you're worse than, well, Katie Hopkins . . .

Most people on the dole don't choose to be there, absolutely not. But those who do hardly cost the country anything, don't really do any harm and lead quite a dull and boring life.

And let's face it, there are people who should never be allowed near any sort of job owing to their massive capacity to fuck it up. I can think of plenty of geezers who are much safer sitting at home smoking dope and watching *Loose Women* than they are being a road sweeper or khazi attendant. I wouldn't want to use a khazi they'd attended, that's for sure, it'd stink and they'd be selling weed out the back of it. I swear some of them could fuck it up so badly someone would die. They couldn't even be criminals. They're the sort who would ram-raid Oxfam. Slinging 'em a bullseye a week's cheap compared to the mayhem they might cause left to fend for themselves.

The whole country, all of us, needs to learn to live and let live a bit.

20

I could have done with lying a bit more in my life but I'm not about to start. If you lie you are a traitor to yourself. You may think you are lying to get what you want, but unless what you want is to be a slag, don't lie.

When you're asked what you think of someone you've got two ways to go. You can say you love everyone, all tits and teeth – and you've got my way.

I could have done with lying a bit more in my life but I'm not about to start. If you lie you are a traitor to yourself. You may think you are lying to get what you want, but unless what you want is to be a slag, don't lie.

By lying I mean not being true to yourself. I could have got on a lot better if sometimes, when people asked me what I thought of some actor or another, I'd said, 'He's a great bloke,' as opposed to 'He's a proper melt.' In retrospect, I might have sucked up to people like Guy Ritchie more but he rubbed me up the wrong way so I mugged him off.

If I'd grovelled a bit more I might have got a lot more work but bollocks. I'm an actor for a living, I don't bring it home with me. At home I'm who I am and I couldn't live with myself if I wasn't.

This caused me trouble when I was younger – I'd say my opinions and I was advised to shut the north and south. But there are enough tarts out there, desperate for success, desperate for fame, who reduce themselves to jelly moulds. I ain't gonna do it.

It's ridiculous to tell yourself that you can only be happy if you fulfil certain dreams.

It's easy to lie to yourself. A lot of people do that but I try not to. I see some actors, for instance, who because they play hard men roles, start to believe they're hard men. That ain't me. I'm a softy, really.

Also, because you've got a talent for something you can start to believe you're something special, deserve different treatment from other people. That ain't the way to go.

This sounds a load of schmaltzy rubbish but the biggest lie you can tell yourself is 'I can't do it'. That gets drummed into some people so they never try anything different or find out where their talents lie. All right, there are limits – I ain't ever gonna make it with the Royal Ballet even if I wanted to but I think you need to go for your dreams.

I've felt inadequate and scared myself, of course I have. When I was on Jonathan Ross's show, walking on to the set, I don't remember at all getting out of the chair. They called me and, as I stood up, I felt this huge rush of fear. There's so much that can go wrong on those programmes. You can look like you're trying too hard, you have to be witty, but you have to watch what you say. You are in a room with a lot of famous people like Liam Neeson and Goldie Hawn and that's the pressure in itself. So as I got to my feet, I just thought, 'I can't do this.' I thought I was going to faint. Really, I thought I might just drop on the floor there and then.

I'd had such a bad run and it had all turned around so miraculously that I thought something had to go wrong. I don't remember the walk to the seat. But then when I sat down I thought, 'He's a human being, I'm a human being, I can do this.' The

I ain't ever gonna make it with the Royal Ballet even if I wanted to but I think you need to go for your dreams.

crowd gave me a very nice reception and that relaxed me. Really I was just afraid of fear. I know what I'm capable of, I can sit with Jonathan Ross, whatever he wants to throw at me, if he wants to go to work with me I'll go to work with him. It was just that moment as I stood up. What if I had fainted? Maybe it would have been all right, Tony Soprano used to collapse.

But I had to walk through that gate of fear in order to get to the garden on the other side, if you see what I mean.

On the other hand, it's ridiculous to tell yourself that you can only be happy if you fulfil certain dreams, particularly if they involve getting a load of material possessions. You can be happy by just getting love in your life, which is free.

When I was having a hard time I started to tell myself that I couldn't be happy if I didn't get back to the top of my game. Was that really true? I'd still have had my kids, Jo, and my memories. That'd do me. Life would have been very different, for sure, but who knows in ten or twenty years where I would have been? I might have been in a better place.

It's hard not to lie to ourselves sometimes, because lies protect us. But if you look at yourself with truth and honesty, most of us will find we've got more than we think.

21

Those who do not remember the mistakes of the past are fucked, in my opinion.

I love a conspiracy theory, me. Years ago you might have laughed at people who claimed the world was one big carve-up but now, who knows?

Every time you turn on the TV there's some rich old man being hauled over the coals for some sort of skulduggery. They're all at it – FIFA, the EU, the lot. They reckon corruption in the EU costs £99 billion a year. And these are the melts who want more control of our budgets. I bet they do.

Other conspiracies really fascinate me. Take 9/11. Some people say there's more to that than meets the eye. I don't know, though I've seen stuff that might make me doubt the explanation we were given. The real point, though, is that we've lost so much trust in our governments that we find it hard to believe anything they say.

I mean, if you take what they say as true, then the train of events don't add up. Osama Bin Bell End smashes the planes into the towers, hides out in Pakistan, about ten feet from a military academy and we respond by invading Iraq, a country that seemingly had nothing to do with 9/11, at the same time as licking the arse of Saudi Arabia. If that's a plot for a film, it's gonna get chucked back at the writer because it don't make sense.

Why don't we have a go at the Saudis? Because they play the game of inviting in Western companies to do loads of expensive work for them, making sure the oil money goes back into western economies. That buys them a pass to do what they like – finance terrorism, cut off people's heads, keep women like slaves. Try to keep that money in your own country and you'll see the tanks roll in. Does anyone honestly believe Saddam – who was a cunt – was removed because of weapons of mass destruction? No, he just didn't hand his money over to the US corporations to get them to build a load of expensive shit like the Saudis did. So bang, off he went. The West would have put up with any of his tricks if the money had kept rolling in.

Every time you turn on the TV there's some rich old man being hauled over the coals for some sort of skullduggery.

If the government are spending so much on surveillance – they know virtually every time you run out of bread nowadays – why didn't they manage to work out that Osama Bin Laden was shacked up in sight of the military who were meant to be hunting him? Who is working for the security services? Mr Bean? I don't think he is. So is there another explanation for why he was missed?

Bin Liner was pretty useful while he was alive – he justified massive military spending, nose poking on a massive scale, the invasion of big oil fields. Around the time they topped him, Al-Qaida was losing power and other, even more mad organizations were appearing. Maybe the West didn't need him any more.

I'm not saying all this is right – the true account may be exactly as the powers that be have said it is. But there are some difficult questions for them to answer.

I cannot bend my nut around it but whatever's going on don't add up to me.

We're rightly meant to be up in arms about ISIS and the atrocities of these terrorist slags but we hold a UN Human Rights conference in Saudi Arabia – a country which beheads more people than ISIS and where you can't get your missus to drive you home if you've had a skin full. It's a place of massive wealth but if you're some poor mug who can't afford to eat and you steal something, they chop off your hands. Then they fuck off back to their palaces in their gold-plated Rolls-Royces or whatever they drive. We're not supposed to care about that because they buy so many arms from us.

The government tells us we're under massive threat. Are we? We didn't have all this surveillance and stuff when the IRA were blowing up half of Canary Wharf, and Al-Qaida have managed very little in this country by comparison. Let me be totally clear. I'm not down-playing the events of 7/7, which was awful and an outrage, but the IRA were a deadlier foe. You might say that's because of surveillance but there's plenty of countries who don't spend that money who've been relatively all right.

And if we're turning into a surveillance state because of them, aren't we giving up the freedoms we're meant to be defending?

At the time of writing, oil prices are dropping. Why aren't the Saudis moving to protect them? They say it's just business but plenty of people think strings are being pulled to hurt Putin. Putin gets a lot of bad press but in the last thirty years the Russians have given up huge territories without a shot being fired while we've been stomping about bombing every mug who sticks his head out of a hole.

What's going on in Ukraine? Fuck knows. What I do know is that it's none of our business. Imagine if Russia started sending a massive amount of money to a British revolutionary movement – which is effec-tively what the West is doing in Ukraine. We'd go mental. There are parts of the US that want independence. What would happen if Putin bunged the old Confederate states a few billion roubles to tool up?

I have three words for what's going on, and I admit this may be influenced by too much late-night TV but they're these: New World Order. I honestly believe there is an international gang of rich slags trying to take over the world, through corporations, through trade treaties, and it's trying to bypass the power of countries. Putin won't have it.

How we've got the right to call him out for aggression is beyond me. They call Russia a gangster economy. They say Putin carved up the state and sold it off to his mates. So what is

We've lost so much trust in our governments that we find it hard to believe anything they say.

George Osborne doing? What did Maggie Thatcher do with the British press – and aren't we living with the fallout from that sly move?

Now I know Putin isn't exactly Gandhi but I reckon we should have learned enough in Iraq to know that, when we get rid of someone we don't like, we might end up with someone we like a lot less instead. Again, it does my nut in. Anyone who thinks about this for ten minutes can see it but we plough on doing the same things again and again.

Those who do not remember the mistakes of the past are fucked, in my opinion.

22

There are blokes throwing themselves down hills in the Peak District today on full suspension mountain bikes who have Germaine Greer to thank for them.

Feminism is the posh word for girl power. Equality of the sexes, all that. I think it's a wonderful thing. It's done amazing things for my life.

You take my career. For quite a while, like a lot of actors, I've been skint and out of work. During that time I relied on Joanne – she was working as a financial adviser. If she hadn't been able to get an education – she somehow dragged ten GCSEs out of the school we went to – and get a decent job, I wouldn't have had the platform to follow my dreams.

Feminism has been *very, very* good for blokes, in fact much better than it's been for birds.

That's not to knock what it's done for birds, of course, because it's done great things. It put them on equal, or equal-ish, wages to men, opened up careers that had previously been closed to them and meant that they no longer had to get married if they wanted to leave their mum and dad's house. In my mum's generation, and even more so in my nan's, a girl moved out of her parents' only when she started to live with her husband.

The treacles could earn their own wedge and they were in less of a rush to get hitched. This was great for men – I see it all around me. All right, I shacked up early but a lot of blokes I know were still shagging like rabbits at an age at which a lot of their dads would have been married for years.

Best of all, women could suddenly admit to being interested in sex, talk about it, swap tips. Birds in the fifties used to ask, 'Does he bother you much?' By the eighties they was getting pissed on Lambrini at Ann Summers parties and menacing their fellas with all manner of plastic objects. Some of 'em were coming to East End pubs and outraging the decency of the common man for money, as we have seen above. Things were going on in dockers' bedrooms that, a couple of generations before, were only encountered in Bangkok knocking shops. You no longer had to join the Merchant Navy to experience that sort of thing, which was a relief for those of us who suffer from sea sickness.

A bird with her own job is a cheaper date too. She shares the bill for meals and nights out and the man comes away at the end of the month with a fat wodge of cash still left in his pocket.

What to spend it on? Havin' it, in various ways, whatever takes your fancy. Take a look at the ads in a lad mag – motorbikes, kite surfing, skiing, extreme sports – and plain old getting pissed. There are blokes throwing themselves down hills in the Peak District today on full suspension mountain bikes who have Germaine Greer to thank for them.

Sometimes I think feminism has been bad for women. I'm lucky, I can afford to keep my family without Joanne needing to work now and she wants to concentrate on the family. Plenty of modern birds go out to work, put the dinner on the table so to speak, and then clear the table and wash up. She's scrubbing the floor while the bloke flicks through *FHM* deciding which gadget to buy with the money her income has freed up.

It's difficult to think of many areas where feminism hasn't benefited men. Oh yes, those dungarees radical feminists used to wear. They were horrible.

Feminism has made family life sweeter too. Blokes have to pitch in with the kids nowadays, which means they have a bond-up with them.

I do try to help with the kids, get involved, be around for them. I think the previous generations of men, who had less to do with childcare, were missing out really.

I love to watch films with my kids – I was watching *Cinderella* with Sunnie the other day and I have to say, a tear came to my eye when the glass slipper went on her little trotter ... Poor cow. Obviously, I wouldn't sit down and watch *Cinderella* on my own but with Sunnie it's a nice little moment.

It just wouldn't have entered the nut of men of my granddad's generation that they might spend a morning pushing a swing in a playground while their wives had coffee with their friends.

And, today, of course, there's the expectation that women and men will share more. It's not him in the shed and her in the kitchen with her cakes. Women demand more from the fellas and that's made us better people.

In fact, it's difficult to think of many areas where feminism hasn't benefited men. Oh yes, those dungarees radical feminists used to wear. They were horrible. There was a point when women couldn't admit to liking make-up and a nice frock. All that stuff was just the birth pangs of a brighter, more beautiful world, though, the world of today – a man's world – made and shaped by the women's movement. Blokes should be thankful for it.

23

I think it's important that we believe UFOs exist anyway. It gives us a bit of perspective, stops us gazing up our own arseholes and means we think of something a bit more meaningful than who's nabbed me parking space at the supermarket and how house prices are doing.

A lot of people take the piss out of me over UFOs. Some of these same people have no problem at all talking about God or Jesus or whoever. Well, the way I look at it, if there's a God, there has to be aliens, don't there? You can't say, 'There's this invisible bloke no one has ever seen, yet aliens – who lots of people have seen – don't exist.'

I think it's important that we believe UFOs exist anyway. It gives us a bit of perspective, stops us gazing up our own arseholes and means we think of something a bit more meaningful than who's nabbed me parking space at the supermarket and how house prices are doing.

Think about it. Astronomers reckon that, just in our neck of the woods – the Milky Way – there could be thirty billion inhabitable worlds.

If you want to really get your nut blown apart, get hold of this. Astronomers reckon that for every grain of sand on earth, there are 10,000 stars out there. In the whole universe there are 500 billion billion Sun-like stars and one hundred billion billion Earth-like planets.

No aliens on that lot? Do one.

Again, the astronomers have had a little count up and reckon we have 100,000 intelligent civilizations in our galaxy alone.

And the *New Scientist* says, 'The chances that we're alone in the cosmos seem very slim, indeed.'

Then there's NASA – remember them, walking on the moon, all that? They say we will find signs of alien life within twenty years.

So next time you see me on the telly talking about UFOs and think, 'What a melt,' remember that *New Scientist* journalists, who have a shedload of PhDs and all that, agree with me. There's an army of boffins behind me. Take me on and Stephen Hawking's got my back. Yeah, sceptics, you're all for it when you think you can get all over Danny Dyer about it. Hawking turns up and you don't want to know.

Governments take this shit seriously. There is a load of scientific activity called SETI (search for extra terrestrial intelligence). The only problem is that, so far, they have encountered exactly nothing. They're looking for radio signals but they've found nothing. Brussels sprout. Why?

This is where it gets proper mental and I turn to the internet. There's a good website called 'waitbutwhy' that explains all this in more detail but I'll put it in laymelt's terms.

Our sun – which is a star like lots of others – is quite young. There are lots of other stars like it which are a lot older, some by billions of years.

So any aliens on these worlds could have a three to four billion year head start on us. You think how much technology has come on just in my lifetime and you might see how, if they don't want to be noticed, they won't be noticed.

Why wouldn't they want to be noticed? Well, we don't go marching into the middle of the Amazon any more, looking to dig out undiscovered people, it's seen as bad karma. Maybe they're on the same trip. Or maybe they just can't be arsed. Why would they want to invade us? With 100 billion billion other planets to choose from, why bother coming down here for a tear-up. It's not like real estate's in short supply. I like the idea of an alien up there saying, 'Shall we go and

Sceptics, you're all for it when you think you can get all over Danny Dyer about it. Hawking turns up and you don't want to know.

invade Earth?' and another saying, 'Bollocks, I'm off down the inter-galactic boozer.'

Have we lost contact with a 'mother civilization'? Is there some reason we're left to develop alone? Maybe the sheer size of the universe means that the geezer responsible for looking after us has just got too much to do. Maybe he's just lazy, been forced into taking the job of Earth Guardian by the Cosmic Job Centre but prefers just to have a pint and let us get on with it. But is our whole purpose as a species to develop space travel? And if so, why are some slags fucking around with war and all that shit?

Other people have different views summed up by the saying that explains why we've heard nothing, which is 'We're rare, we're first or we're fucked.'

This says that there's a 'great filter', an evolutionary stage beyond which it's very hard to go. Most species don't make it down from the trees, say. We're an exception. Maybe the big leap comes in there being life at all. Maybe we're the only ones who made that leap into life. That don't explain UFOs, though, does it? Where do they come from, if we're alone?

We could be first. That is, the big evolutionary leap has just happened. The conditions in most places just weren't right for it in the past and we're the first intelligent civilization to emerge.

Or we could be fucked. The big evolutionary leap is in front of us and we might not make it. An asteroid, a burst of space radiation or one of these public schoolboys kicking off a war might do us all in.

I wouldn't be surprised here because, with the number of slags about with nuclear weapons, chemical and biological stuff, it'll only take one of them to lose it and we're dead. Is that as far as any civilization can get – the development of weapons of mass destruction? So that means the biggest threat to humanity is its own governments. They're the ones with the bombs.

There is a shedload of other reasons we might not have heard anything.

Maybe we're too primitive to understand communications. Maybe the minds of other civilizations are faster or slower than ours and the communications are pinched into nanoseconds or stretched over centuries. Or maybe they're forbidden from making contact with lower life forms, like in *Star Trek*. Flying saucers might be like lads on a stag night, nipping down here for a naughty thrill scaring the shit out of military pilots.

I think that maybe we're like jellyfish in the sea. We know as much about alien civilizations as the jellyfish do about ours.

I'm certain that UFOs exist.

Not all the evidence for UFOs is as bang on as a believer like me might hope. For instance, a lot of early sightings have been put down to blips with the early days of radar. That is, radar operators didn't always understand what they were seeing – atmospheric conditions and all that jive.

And let's face it, the world is full of nutters and liars. Some people will do anything to get on TV and some people are just crazy.

However, some cases are right on it. Wrap your nut around this one. In 1952 British forces took part in an operation called 'Mainbrace' – designed to prepare us for Soviet attack. (Seems the scaremongerers were out in force back in the day too. If the Soviets couldn't get a jar of jam into a supermarket, they sure as shit weren't going to invade Western Europe.)

During this, all the top brass – that's military generals and whatever, not leading prostitutes – were invited to come and look at an air display up at Topcliffe, which is in the north somewhere. Don't ask me, anything past Watford's like Narnia to me.

The UFO appeared, *during the display*! There are records of the top boys at the RAF saying that it was as clear as the nose on Zlatan Ibrahimović's face.

That one was all over the papers but another one got hushed up. This was at an RAF gaffe called Little Rissington in Gloucestershire. An RAF pilot called Michael Swiney was giving a lesson to a student pilot in a Meteor jet.

They saw, clearly and right in front of them, three UFOs the shape of the bottom of a wine glass – long and flat. The UFO was clocked by two pilots, both of who checked to see they weren't tripping off on lack of oxygen or nothing like that.

The pilot said, 'I had then been flying for about nine years and I had seen many funny reflections, refractions through windscreens and lots of other things, but this was nothing of the sort. We tried very hard to explain away what we were looking at but there was no way we could do that. There was something there, there is absolutely no doubt about it. It was NOT a reflection.'

On top of this, the radar crew down below clocked 'em as well – doing 3,000 miles per hour. They were so worried, they scrambled a couple of armed jets.

Mr Swiney has always stuck to his story. He wasn't some tripped-out hippy – he finished up as Air Commodore, that's like a Brigadier in the Army. He had quite a lot to lose by saying what he saw – people might not take him seriously, he might have been overlooked for promotion. But it didn't knock him back.

Then there was the Rendlesham Forest incident. In this, US Air Force personnel – including the base commander – encountered UFOs in the woods outside the airbase. There had been a report of a UFO the night before and the base commander thought it was bollocks so he set out to knock it on the head lively.

He got a lot more than he bargained for.

On the tape he says, 'I see it too . . . it's back again . . . it's coming this way . . . there's no doubt about it . . .

this is weird . . . it looks like an eye winking at you . . . it almost burns your eyes . . . he's coming toward us now . . . now we're observing what appears to be a beam coming down to the ground – one object still hovering over Woodbridge base . . . beaming down.'

He later signed a legal declaration to swear – on pain of losing his nuts – what he said was true. His men even had an encounter with an alien, they documented the lot. Would the base commander really want to lie about this? The amount of paperwork alone must have been enough to put him off.

We should be looking to the stars, not rolling in the gutter, kicking each other in the Davina McCalls.

Also, he launched his own investigation into the case and found British radar had picked up odd objects in the vicinity. And, to me, the statement put out by the Ministry of Defence sounds very iffy. They say, 'There was no threat to UK security.' That's not 'there were no UFOs', is it?

So eat that, ya sceptical mugs, ya!

There's a lot more detail on this stuff on the website of a geezer called Dr David Clarke.

Now we've proved there are UFOs, this brings us on to an important question.

What are aliens like? Weird-looking fuckers, that's what. Big eyes. I saw one on a video made by Stan Romanek – a bloke who says he's been abducted hundreds of times. He was a weird character – but he showed me a film we weren't able to show on the BBC because of the amount of money he wanted for it. It's the most incredible thing I've ever seen, an alien poking its head round a door, long fingers, bug eyes. Either that bloke has access to CGI – which would cost a lot of money – or it's real.

Romanek was arrested for child porn last year – which he says was planted on him by the government. Obviously if he's a nonce, he deserves to be put in a rocket and shot into space. Abduct the slag and don't bring him back, please aliens. I didn't clock him for one, but then again they're very good at hiding it, aren't they? But it will make an interesting scientific experiment if he gets locked up. If he finishes up on the roof of the prison – like he said he did at home after being abducted – I guess everyone will have to admit he's being abducted.

If the aliens come for him again and take him out of prison, at least we'll know he wasn't bullshitting. If his claims are true and he's been set up as a sex monster, this could be the silver lining for him. There again, there's no reason aliens shouldn't abduct sex cases too. Maybe that's why they're poking probes up people's arses, trying to understand these sickos. I suppose it would make quite a good title for his biography: 'Interstellar Nonce'. This kind of thing poisons everything. How can anyone now watch *Star Trek: The Next Generation* without thinking of some horrible double meaning?

Some scientists think aliens might look just like us, though. Evolution only goes one way, they say. If you want a flying warm-blooded creature, it's gonna look like a bird, a flower is the most efficient way of doing what a flower does, we are the most efficient way of carrying a relatively big brain about.

This means there could be drawings of aliens all over the shop and we wouldn't see them. What about those whacky hieroglyphs in Egypt – dog-headed men, all that. How do we know they weren't aliens?

Then we come to the pyramids. Back in the day when the pyramids were built, there was no cameras or smart phones or nothing, and the aliens could just come and visit whenever they wanted, and I'm sure they did. We were primitive people then.

There's an amazing aerial shot of the pyramids that shows them like an alien face – incredible. It's clearly an alien's face.

The pyramids are so well aligned with the points of the compass that some people doubt it would even have been possible for the ancient Egyptians to do that without alien help. People back in them days didn't have the technology or the tools to build a pyramid like that. The slope is at such a precise angle. Did some superior being come down and educate people?

They can't come nowadays because of cameras and all that, so they just let us know now and again and go, 'Listen, we are about. Cop for that crop circle, get hold of that, go and debate it.'

Even if this isn't true I like to believe it. It's a sad state of affairs if we're the only intelligent life in the universe.

Alien abductions have to be true, don't they? Again, people piss themselves if I go on about them but there's plenty of very clever bastards who take these cases seriously. There was a conference at MIT – a major US university – one year. *The New Yorker* magazine sent a bloke along to write a column taking the piss and he came back a complete believer.

The first ever case was of a bloke called Antônio Vilas-Boas, not to be confused with the old Chelsea and Spurs manager who the fans were praying would get abducted. They had big signs outside his house with 'ET, this way' written on 'em.

This Antônio was working on a farm at night in his field and was taken up and shagged by a big-eyed cat-like alien. It was confirmed he had burns all over his body.

Since then there have been thousands of cases. Some of them – like one where a nurse was abducted by praying mantis-type creatures – are really convincing.

The bloke researching it mentioned the case to a mate of his in the same game. This other bloke had two cases in the same place reporting exactly the same thing.

How do you explain something like that? No communication between any of them.

Like I said, I totally believe in aliens. And, even if they didn't exist, it wouldn't do no one no harm to think they did. We should be looking to the stars, not rolling in the gutter, kicking each other in the Davina McCalls.

24

I quite like the Queen, it's more the institution that could do with a bit of scrutiny.

I'm in two minds about the royal family. I'm very proud to be British, very proud to be a Londoner and I'm fascinated by all their history, how the bloodline goes back generations.

Mind you, London hasn't always had a great relationship with the royal family. Apparently, there was times in the medieval period when the king had to ask permission to enter the city. Sometimes the king had to lock himself in the Tower of London to protect himself from the city mob. The city viewed itself as a country of its own. I think there's a little bit about it like that today.

There's a rumour in my family that we are descended from the poet John Milton. Now I've no idea if that's true but maybe there's something in the DNA that makes us suspicious of royalty. Milton was one of the most important geezers in English history, certainly one of the most important thinkers. He was the bloke who wrote the justification for the execution of

Charles I, so the relationship between my family and the royals has a bit of history. I have no idea whether this is true but it would make me laugh if it was. He was born in Cheapside apparently, so not too far at all.

Stick that up your Lycidas, poncy critics!

Anyway, I digress. I think it's great what the Queen represents to foreign countries – all that history. There's nothing quite like that in the world, well you have sheikhs and other kings and queens but nothing on that level, so internationally renowned. So that makes me very proud. And it's brilliant that in London you can see modern buildings right next to a palace, there's nowhere quite like that.

That said, I ask myself how much we get from them for the money we pay. And sometimes, they do take the piss. I read that the Queen applied to the poverty fund to get the money to heat Buckingham Palace. A bit naughty. They should pay for their own maintenance.

I'm not sure I know exactly what the royal family do. I'd certainly like to drop their money, and let them go and earn money. I wouldn't get rid of them. They are a massive part of being British, you can't deny that.

I would like to meet the Queen though, to have that moment. I don't know if I could do the protocol, do the little curtsy. You have to call her ma'am to rhyme with 'jam', not to rhyme with 'arm'. Don't say 'marm', for fuck's sake, you'll be beheaded.

I respect William, because he went and got a trade. He can fly a helicopter, so you've got to hold your hands up to that. I love Harry. He really did break the mould. Apparently his nickname was Hash Harry at Eton. The others are a bit wishy washy really. Edward is a nonentity. Then there's Andrew, and we're getting into tricky territory there.

Should we keep them? Purely for tourist reasons. I don't really think they fit with the modern age and it's a big ask for them really. They'd probably be happier out of the public eye.

I'm not a royalist in any shape or form, though.

One thing I don't understand is the media portrayal of the royal family. Take the coverage of the royal babies. Nowhere do we have, say, an estimate of how much the new baby is costing the taxpayer every day in protection, housing, transport, all that. Instead we have photographers stuck outside a hospital – I have no idea what they expect to see outside a hospital – rabitting on about absolutely nothing. Nothing at all. 'Ah, a raindrop, dropping. Ploosh. Still no news.' Christ, it was shit.

It was all over the news, but there was no news. At all. Even when the baby was born. 'The baby has been born.' OK, fine. Now what? You'd think it would stop there but they keep giving it some for the next two days. 'What will Kate be thinking at this time?' 'What would your advice be for William?' Is anyone that interested in it? Come down a boozer in the East End, then and ask what the birth of the royal baby means to the people there, what effect it will have on their lives. 'Fuck all,' would be the general answer, I would guess. They don't hate the royal family, far from it, but I just don't think they give them that much thought. The pubs weren't full of people waiting to toast the new baby into the world.

I heard Prince Philip's comment on *EastEnders* was, 'I don't understand all the misery. Your Cockney's a chirpy fellow, isn't he?' That, to me, shows how out of touch they are with normal people's lives. Mind you, I quite admire Prince Philip, at least he says what he thinks.

You don't hear any talk about how those poor kids are going to live their lives, with a telephoto lens shoved up their nappy. Basically, how their lives are going to be shit apart from being minted, which is always a bonus.

What I also don't get is that we're meant to be excited by the whole thing. That does baffle me. Why? I honestly do not know. Maybe no one told me some big secret when I was growing up, maybe everyone else knows something I don't. It's a kid. Lovely. Thanks for that. Now show us a dog on a skateboard.

I appreciate the royals are in a difficult bind. The public want them to be normal but at the same time they have to be something more than normal. I know I've talked about fame but their level of fame is unbelievable and the way the Queen deals with that for so long is commendable. I thought it was brave of her to do the Northern Ireland trip.

Personally, I quite like the Queen, it's more the institution that could do with a bit of scrutiny. I'm sure she's just a normal human being. She gets that dress and hat off, and slips on her Care Bear nightie. I like the idea of that normality.

Of course, they're all recovering from their terrible treatment of Princess Diana. I do believe Diana was killed. I don't know who did it, or why they did it, but in my bones I feel there was some sort of skulduggery going on there. There are all sorts of theories about who and why, and I doubt we'll ever know what really went on.

I'm sure the Queen's just a normal human being. She gets that dress and hat off, and slips on her Care Bear nightie. I like the idea of that normality.

Some people have claimed that the security forces were just trying to warn her, to show her what might happen if she didn't play the game by dumping her knocky boyfriend.

It does seem too much like a coincidence that her boyfriend Dodi was about to propose to her – it's said that he'd bought a ring. Not only was he a Muslim, he was the son of Mohamed Al Fayed, someone the British establishment fucking hated.

There are also rumours that Diana was pregnant – photos of her taken on a beach seemed to show her with a bit of a bump. Was she? She'd have had to be quick because she'd only been going out with him for a short while. But that's the rumour. If she had married Dodi and gone abroad with him, with William and Harry, the British establishment would have dropped a bollock.

One thing's for sure – the whole thing is murky.

There's a few things I personally find incredible about her death. The first is that it happened in a tunnel – where no mobile phones would work. No one could have made an emergency call to say they were being harassed, no one could see what went on.

Also, witnesses have said that her car was being followed by two other cars and a motorbike. The cars were harassing Diana's car through the tunnel. The witnesses said that the motorbike flashed something into Diana's driver's face. Then the motorcyclist pillion passenger jumped off the bike, looked at the crash and crossed his arms – a military sign for 'mission accomplished'.

Now the paparazzi were chasing her but they were acquitted of causing her death in a French court. They say they didn't get to the tunnel until a minute after the crash and the courts seem to back them on that.

So who was in the car and on the motorbike – both seen by many witnesses. There have been rumours the SAS were involved, but I can't believe a British regiment would assassinate a British princess. MI6 have been named. Is that possible?

There are still questions to be answered, I think. Lord Stevens – the geezer who headed up the British inquiry into the crash – said the driver Henri Paul was not pissed at the time he lost control of the car, at least when he spoke to Paul's parents. In his official report, he maintained that the driver had been drunk. Also, considering that the most famous woman in the world had just died, there was a massive cock-up when it came to analysing Paul's blood samples. You'd think that, if there was ever a time to be a bit careful, it would have been then.

Then there was a paparazzi photographer, who has been linked to MI6, who was meant to be driving one of the cars right behind Diana on the night, though he denied it. He was found in a remote woodland, shot in the head in a burnt-out car three years after the crash. His family are convinced it wasn't suicide – they say that he'd just got a new job and was over the moon about it.

They say the car that Dodi and Di were in was speeding. But Dodi's ex-girlfriends say he hated going fast and they used to take the piss out of him for driving at forty miles per hour on country roads. Would he let his chauffeur drive quickly?

Then there's the letter Diana wrote predicting her own death, specifically saying that she feared a car crash. Lord Mischon – a solicitor who helped her with her divorce, said she was convinced there was a conspiracy to get rid of her.

He wrote a note that said she was afraid: 'Efforts would be made if not to get rid of her (be it by some accident in her car, such as a pre-prepared brake failure or whatever) at least to see she was so injured as to be declared unbalanced.'

There's too much suspicious stuff around this death, too many coincidences and conflicting stories. Will we ever know the truth? I doubt it.

25

The football authorities have done very little to protect fans, the FA in particular. But it's the fans who will rescue the game and, I think, it's the fans that could breathe new life into the national team.

Why haven't we won the World Cup since my dad was a nipper? Why haven't we even got close since I was thirteen? That was the last time England got to the semis of a major competition.

Two letters – FA, and you know what that stands for – fuck all. If you take away the World Cup and a couple of flash-in-the-pan tournaments, our record in international competition, right from the start, is appalling.

People talk about bringing through English players. But the clubs have so much money they won't play them. You want to benefit the England team? Then the Premier League needs to make it a priority, but they never will because each club's looking after its own.

There are massive stumbling blocks preventing us doing what needs to be done. The Premier League is too powerful and the FA are toothless.

What's required? Legislation. The government are quick enough to claim they are football supporters when it suits them – though, unlike David Cameron, I have never mistaken West Ham for Aston Villa. Now they need to step in and save the game.

There was a report by a group in parliament that gave an ultimatum to the people running the game – get it sorted or we will. I don't know what happened to that, we never seemed to hear of it again, even though the report gave the FA and the like twelve months to act and that was 2013.

The government needs to make laws to give the game back to the fans. It's too important to hand the destiny of our national game to a bunch of foreign owners. I'm sure the Qataris and Roman Abramovich and the Glazers are lovely fellas, but do they really give a flying for what happens to the England team?

And look what happened at Hull, some geezer coming in and saying they were going to be called 'Tigers'. This ain't America where owners can just move a team from a city or change its name and the fans will swallow it. This is England. The club doesn't belong to the bloke whose name is on the deeds, it belongs to the fans. They are the club. It always has been and should remain a working man's sport.

The football authorities have done very little to protect fans, the FA in particular. But it's the fans who will rescue the game and, I think, it's the fans that could breathe new life into the national team.

Some of the stuff that's gone on has been outrageous. At Cardiff City, the owner, Vincent Tan, changed the kit from blue to red, so it would sell better in the Far East. Gobsmacking. How could the FA allow that?

Then there were Tom Hicks and George Gillett Jr at Liverpool. How were they ever allowed to take over a club like that? They rode up massive debts at the club without increasing its value and managed to sell it at an enormous loss. They had no feeling for the fans whatever. If they can do that to Liverpool, who is safe?

Worse than that were the couple of melts who took over Wrexham. They made an agreement which read: 'The management and control of [Wrexham] Football Club is to be on an equal control basis with the main and sole objective to realise the maximum potential gain from the property assets of the Football Club for the benefit of Alex Hamilton and Mark Guterman.' It's enough to make your blood run cold. They bought the club with the idea of trying to make themselves rich and to flog it off as a retail park. It was left to the courts to sort that one out. The football authorities stood by shrugging their shoulders.

The Welsh FA, if anything, seems worse than the English. They let Barry Town be taken over by Stuart Lovering. All right, it wasn't immediately obvious he was a bell end but when your chairman talks about playing himself in a key match in your fight against relegation, you know something's up.

He actually just took the club out of the league. No reason, just withdrew it. And the Welsh FA let him. It took a judge to restore sense.

Winning when your team has an injection of outside money is like storming a video game with all the cheats running. It's fun, but is it satisfying?

I could go on. In fact, I will. The authorities allowed Wimbledon to be bought and sold to Milton Keynes like it was a second-hand motor. They allowed Darlington to be sold to an ex-safe cracker who built a 25,000-seater stadium to house the club's 1,000 average attendance and who drove it into non-existence. Then there's Leeds with Peter Ridsdale – spend, spend, spend, oops, the wheel's come off. I miss Leeds. The Premier League's not the same without them to hate.

What's Mike Ashley doing at Newcastle? Bringing in Dennis Wise! I think a Mackem Satan would have been more popular.

If fans had been more involved, if they'd owned the clubs, none of this would have happened. You can't see Wimbledon saying, 'I'll tell you what, boys, let's play in Milton Keynes,' or Barry Town fans saying, with two games of the season to go, 'I've had enough of this football lark. Let's fold up the club and go bowling.' The football authorities have done nothing to prevent any of this.

The impact of foreign owners over here has been bad too. The game starts to become like Formula 1 – a contest between bank accounts.

So what needs to be done? If in doubt, look to the teams and the leagues with the most success. Who are they? Germany.

I know it sticks in the throat to have to take lessons from the nation of Rudi Völler and the depressingly good penalty shoot-out but they have a lot to teach us.

First and foremost, the collective good outweighs any individual needs. What's better for the German team is more important than what's important for any one club. I can almost see you shaking your head and saying, 'What planet are you on, Dan?' But it's true. This is how they do it: in Germany they have the fifty plus one rule. That means the club members have to own over half of the shares in the club.

That would make an enormous difference to the club's priorities. Fans care about the national side, would want to see home-grown players come through. Fans also care about the prices. When Borussia Dortmund played Arsenal, the club was so mugged off by the ticket prices that it bought the entire allocation and sold them to its fans at half price. That club cares about the fans.

In England, particularly in the Premiership, you sometimes get the idea the clubs think it's a privilege for you to come and watch them and that you should pay a high price for it. In some clubs the fans are seen as little more than background colour to make the match look good on TV.

Give the fans the power!

Now that might mean that player wages had to be reduced. And then the best players in the world might not want to come here. I mean, who'd be bothered to even lace their boots for a measly £50,000 a week? But do these superstars really come here anyway? I'd say only the top five or six clubs get the very best players with the rest fighting for scraps.

I wouldn't regard it as a tragedy if Man City, Chelsea and all the rest had to rely on their support more for their income. And do fans want to see all the best players? Well, it's nice but there's more to it than that. We want to see our team win. How's that going to happen for West Ham or – remember this – Nottingham Forest, or Everton? Gary Glitter's got more chance of a comeback while we're operating the present rules. Fan power wouldn't completely take away the big boys' advantage but it would reduce it quite a lot.

And it would increase everyone's excitement, bring them closer to the action.

Winning when your team has an injection of outside money is like storming a video game with all the cheats running. It's fun, but is it satisfying? What about the clever marshalling of resources, the development of local boys, the old connection between the fan on the terrace and the bloke on the pitch?

The football authorities will not sort it out without a massive kick up the arse. That means outside agencies have to step in. The clubs have had their chance to sort things out, they've been given plenty of warning, now the government should act. The parliamentary report called the Premier League and the FA 'complacent' when it came to including fans. I'll say. To be honest, I sometimes think they'd like to get rid of us altogether and replace us with one big flashing advertising hoarding. And don't get me started on those banner ads that flash round the grounds. Very distracting. I've come to watch football, not be sold a car. In Chinese.

Fans would want to invest in the grassroots game in their area – largely because they play it. Imagine if you heard, instead of a club signing a player for £50 million, they'd just given £50 million to the game in the local area. You may say I'm a dreamer, but I'm not the only melt.

At the moment the whole Premier League contributes £12 million to grassroots football – that's £600,000 each – about three weeks' salary for Eden Hazard, a bit less for Radamel Falcao. It has to change. The clubs exist in a whole football culture and, if they don't recognize that, we need to make them. They should all be contributing much, much more to grassroots football.

The German system makes all the clubs get together with the German FA to have a system of development that goes across the whole nation and isn't tied to any one club.

Owners ain't never gonna do that on their own. It will take the fans' involvement to get investment in young English players and a commitment to bringing them through. If you told me tomorrow West Ham could have Lionel Messi or some raw young talented kid from Custom House, I'd rip your arm off for Messi. Of course I would, I'm not a lunatic. But if you tell me we can have a disappointing non-entity for £9 million – Savio Nsereko, say – I'd say bung £8 million at local development and I'll find you a kid for a oncer. West Ham have a better academy system than most clubs but still we could only benefit from having the grassroots game better funded and better coached.

That's enough football but let me finish on a positive note. Wasn't it nice to see an England team doing so well in the treacle World Cup? It was great to see an England team grow into a tournament, actually surprise us in a good way with their play, their commitment and their passion. That second half against Japan was how I dream of seeing the men's team play. Men of Hodgson: that is how you wear an England shirt. Those lionesses showed desire, gentlemen. Watch and learn. Lionesses are always more powerful than the lion. I would bet my bollocks on it.

No consolation to her, I'm sure, but my player of the tournament was Laura Bassett. Own goals happen to anyone and she was immense in that second half. She reminded me of Bobby Moore and there is no higher praise than that.

26

What's thicker? Having a load of kids, living to party and being surrounded by fun and love, or sweating your youth away on exams to get a job so stressful it will ruin your marriage and kill you by fifty?

I'm a great one for mistakes. They shape you and mature you. Sure, some scar you but so what? You need that if you're to be a fully rounded person.

One of the things that worries me about today's kids is that they're all brought up to be focused on passing exams, getting decent careers, right from when they're small.

Today kids seem over-focused on working hard and preparing for the world of work, rather than enjoying themselves.

I understand why. We live in a fearful time. A lot of people I meet of around my age never had the idea that they wouldn't find it easy to get a good job. Actors could afford to take a punt, knowing it would be fairly straightforward to get back into a proper career later – them who wanted them. Myself, I probably would have just ended up on the dole.

Even for them with no exams there was the reason-able security of a pool of jobs to go back to. All that's out the window today. People don't feel that, if they fall out of the rat race, they can fall back in again.

If you're not settled in a career by the time you're twenty-five, it seems that your life is over. People nowadays seem to see their lives only in terms of their careers. I don't get that at all. To me it's better to be skint, out in the sunshine, breathing the air and free than it is to be shut up doing a job you don't really like.

There are so many other ways to go than grinding away trying to climb the tree, better house, better car, better clothes, always more to want, always more to get. But are they getting what really counts – experi-ence, threat, the opportunity to grow up?

You have kids of twelve talking about careers but they're still stuck at home at thirty. I didn't have a career and I moved out of home when I was sixteen. It's as if they fear the big wide world will bite them, that they'd rather be safely in with mum and dad getting all their laundry done than in a bedsit, independent.

Rebellion seems to have disappeared too. Kids nowadays are all grooving along to Lionel Richie at Glastonbury with their mums and dads. The idea of taking a risk seems to have gone out of things.

What happened to the ideas of becoming an explorer, a pioneer, or someone who just went off to see the world properly – not on a gap year or some charity thing but putting your stick on your shoulder with the sandwich in the hanky on the back and seeing what happens for the next five, ten or twenty years? I was interested in a gap life when I was that age.

Isn't that better than doing a job you half like, living in a place you half like, driving a car you want to get rid of down a road full of thousands of people doing the same?

I know this is easy for me to say because I had a vocation, something I really wanted to do and seemed to be good at. But I've been out of work for long stretches. It never made me think, 'Oh, I wish I'd tried harder at school, wish I'd got a steady job.' I do wish I'd tried harder at school, by the way, not for the exams but for the sake of getting knowledge itself. Being with Harold Pinter was a massive education for me, really shaped me, but it made me realize what an ignorant slag I am.

I'm not knocking steady jobs, not at all. Some people love them, some people have to do them. But if you're doing something that's draining the life from you every day, why not change it? If that means less money, so what?

It's frightening that this wage slavery is the destiny lots of our kids have come to accept as a nailed-on certainty, and as something to aspire to.

I think we are to blame. We've terrified our kids, or some of us have. We've allowed our government to put them through exams from their earliest years, grading them, comparing them, waving the idea of failure over their nuts.

No wonder they turn out as paranoid, conformist wrecks. One survey of young people asked them to describe their lives. The word most often used was 'planned'. Isn't that a bit of a disaster? What happened to taking a risk, standing up for your beliefs?

Miley Cyrus shaking her arse in the air is hardly The Sex Pistols, is it? Maybe the bad boys and girls nowadays are drawn to banking, rather than rebellion.

The only people interested in threatening the status quo are those with nothing to lose – kids from my background. That's why they become criminals or rioters – they can't see a future so they may as well have it right now. That's a destructive and wrong way to behave. But I don't see why we can't harness that energy to good ends.

If you're not plugged into the rat race, if you're happy to make do with what you've got, hanging around, causing no harm but not doing much good, people look down on you, call you a chav. But maybe them 'chavs' – I hate that word – see what it's all about really. People think of them as thick but what's thicker? Having a load of kids, living to party and being surrounded by fun and love, or sweating your youth away on exams to get a job so stressful it will ruin your marriage and kill you by fifty?

The internet, of course, offers an opportunity for people to live life differently. It can be used for great change but it can also give the illusion of action. When you're re-posting some political comment on Facebook, you're either preaching to the converted or arguing with people who will never change their minds.

Music offers no lead. Miley Cyrus shaking her arse in the air is hardly the Sex Pistols, is it? Maybe the bad boys and girls nowadays are drawn to banking, rather than rebellion. It's the place which seems to have no rules, break the code, do things differently. The fact it's a cancer on the planet don't seem to matter.

27

*You can't sell a drug that lowers people's inhibitions
and then complain it lowers their inhibitions.*

There's a lot of hypocrisy around drink. It's a legal
part of our society – something that brings big benefits
to the government through taxes.

Unlike with drugs, there's the idea that, if you end
up as an addict or doing something stupid on drink,
it's your fault. On drugs, it's the fault of the mind-
changing substance you've consumed.

When the old liberal leader Charles Kennedy died
you didn't see any call for the people who had sold
him booze over the years to face jail sentences. There
was no interview with his distraught relatives calling
alcohol evil.

This was despite the fact that the country had lost
one of its most likeable, clever and genuine politicians.

This continues when we get to consider binge drinking. The tabloids, and late-night real-life cop shows,
are always showing some bird with her knickers round
her ankles, lying in a pile of sick while her boyfriend
tries to fight a lamppost.

The tone of these articles is normally that these people are a disgrace, a shame upon the nation. There's the idea that most people go out for a beer and don't end up like that, what's wrong with them that do?

The first thing I wanna ask is this: what is alcohol designed to do? Have a Google on it. Summing it up, it's this: alcohol affects your brain chemistry. Now, what are we, as human beings? A difficult question but the answer is 'our brain chemistry'.

You give someone a drug like that and they start to become someone else. We've all seen it. The smart, funny geezer you meet at eight in the evening's turned into a drooling pig by twelve. He might not be rolling in the street but he ain't so debonair any more, that's for sure.

The thing is, alcohol disinhibits you. That's what it's for, it makes you lose your inhibitions. So you might go out and say, 'I'm having two pints tonight.' You have two pints and the alcohol's affecting you, so you think, 'Bollocks, a third won't hurt.' It's not that you're weak-willed. It's that the drug is designed to do that to you. They'll even give you a helpful range of salty snacks in the pub to make you feel more thirsty. So you have a third. Now you're relaxed, the pool balls are flying in, you feel good. 'Danny, another one?' Of course you're having another one. For a start, it's your round and you can't walk out on your round, can you? So you see, even the way we've set up buying the drinks on the night out subtly encourages you to have more.

OK, four. That's enough. No more than that. 'There you go, Dan, my old son!' There's a pint of lager in front of you. Because it's a round your mate has got one in. Now you've had five pints. To some people that's a skin full. To others it's an aperitif. But one thing's sure, the alcohol is affecting your brain proper now. All your inhibitions are washed away.

I think at this point you're meant to pull out the Drink Aware card and remind yourself you need to be up in the morning. Is that likely to happen? Or are you gonna say: 'Bollocks! If I want to drink, I will drink!'

You can always rely on your inhibitions. Oh no you can't because you've just drowned 'em in five pints.

Now, with experience and age it does become possible to pull out of this binge. You get used to the alcohol, it has less effect on you. Perhaps someone else gives you the red card. Your missus has got round you putting your phone on silent by ringing the pub. Or she's dug your mate's number out of his girlfriend. There are no depths to which these women will not stoop.

So maybe you stop. And, as you get older, you get used to controlling the drug a bit more so you can say, 'That's enough for me.' Or maybe you don't. Maybe it gets its hooks in you and kills you eventually.

When you're eighteen years old, it might be your first time in a bar – kids don't get the slow introduction nowadays, like we used to, what with ID cards and all that pony. Everything in that bar is encouraging you to go for it – two for one deals, the excitement of the music, the feeling of being let off the leash, 'welcome to the house of fun', all that. But that's nothing to the effects of the drug itself. It makes you thirsty, it relaxes you. You could almost say that it's designed to make you want to drink more and more. Maybe you've read a website article about 'getting in the party spirit'. The next morning you'll cure your hangover by reading one of those 'survive the festive blitz' articles.

So you're a young kid and you go for it, no experience of the drug, no way of knowing what your tipping point into being totally blitzed is. The next thing you know, you're vomiting on the pavement outside and the *Daily Mail* have got a camera stuck in your boat. Next day, you're the face of drunken Britain.

My point is this. If you're going to sell the drug at all, what do you expect? You can't sell a drug that lowers people's inhibitions and then complain it lowers their inhibitions. Duh. Yeah.

And ask yourself this, who has the real problem with alcohol? Is it the kids outside the nightclub getting lifted by the Old Bill? Or is it the kids whose mum is plastered on vodka driving them to school, is it the woman who faces her drunken violent husband smashing her about? All the working hours lost to hangovers, the casualty departments banged out with drunks. Some people might never have touched a drink in their lives but they suffer from it.

The people who sell alcohol have done a proper old job on disowning responsibility for what it does. 'You need to be able to hold your beer,' 'You should know when to stop.' Bollocks. It's the drug, it's what it's designed to do. Of a certain number of people who drink, so many will drink too much, so many will commit crime, so many will die. I should think the brewing industry would know the numbers.

The real Queen Vics of the world are precious things and we should hold on to them . . . You're less likely to kick off in a place where the landlady knows your mum.

Imagine if this was applied to drugs. 'The trouble with him is, he couldn't hold his LSD. Finished up in the middle of a traffic island arguing with a daffodil,' or 'The trouble with her is she doesn't know when she's had enough crack cocaine. She should just have one or two pipes and go home.'

I know that sounds ridiculous, but it's how the argument on binge drinking sounds to me. It don't have to be like that every time you go out, but is it any surprise when you end up having ten when you only went out for one?

I love drinking, absolutely love it. I wouldn't be without it for the world. I think it's great fun, most of the time in moderation, occasionally in excess. I don't get lairy, I don't fall over. I just get happy. If I did get in fights, or clump me missus about or drive drunk I'd knock it on the head lively.

Today, the line is that you're meant to enjoy 'a glass or two with friends'. Nothing wrong with that at all. I've enjoyed many evenings on nothing more than a couple of beers.

But let's not bullshit, there's nothing quite as enjoyable as getting on it with a really great bunch of people, having a proper session, a right old knees up as they used to say.

And are you telling me the brewers don't want you to do that? Course they do.

To be able to go for a session like that, you have to have put the work in – like anything, being able to drink a lot is a matter of practice as much as anything else. Try it when you're too young or inexperienced and there will be tears before bedtime.

The kids who are rolling around the floor, being sick and fighting are the equivalent of someone falling off a bike while they're learning to ride it. Yeah, some of them will bang their heads and never wake up. What's the answer? Ban bikes? Or get a training course.

Maybe we should run 'how to get pissed' courses for young people, giving them feedback, showing them videos of themselves, or audio recordings. The thing is, all the advice nowadays is on 'know your limits', know how not to get pissed. How likely is that? About as likely as Rolf Harris being booked for my kids' party. Why not accept people are going to get a right old wet now and again and advise them accordingly, train them to get drunk? This is the brewers' responsibility in my book.

We used to kind of do that. The old boozers were full of older men who'd soon let you know if you was out of order. You didn't need to have your bad behaviour recorded because, believe you me, when you went back in there the next night, everyone would let you know exactly what went on.

Was it better when it was easy to get in a pub from fifteen? You'd sit in there maybe nursing one pint all night because you was too skint to afford any more. By the time you were legal when you were eighteen, maybe earning a bit more, you'd learned how to behave, learned about the effects of alcohol. Not everyone, clearly. But the binge drinking of today that people complain about – which, let's be honest, always went on to a degree – is the result of a whole bunch of people suddenly being let off the lead at the same time.

In the past it wasn't like that, but the natural things that used to hold behaviour in check are going. There aren't as many pubs nowadays where people of all ages go. Pubs seem to have become a bit ghetto-ized, some for young people, some for old. It's a shame – the real Queen Vics of the world are precious things and we should hold on to them. They breed community and they naturally moderate people's behaviour. You're less likely to kick off in a place where the landlady knows your mum.

So next time you see a photo of someone in Marbella slumped in a doorway wearing his underpants for a hat, the headline shouldn't be 'Shame of Britain' but 'Alcohol does what we've known it does for centuries,' or even 'Sure sign of a healthy brewing industry'.

Those kids ain't the problem. The problem is the long-term addicts, the people who are always fighting, who lose their jobs, crash their cars, lose their health. But a bloke with heart failure don't make such a good picture. And, as ever, it doesn't allow the newspaper reader to think in terms of 'us' and 'them'. Look, I'm nothing like that kid, what a disgrace! Let's be fair, a lot of people like nothing better than to feel that way. Maybe they should get treated for binge sneering.

28

I am, in some ways, middle England's nightmare.

I hate the word 'chav'. It's a way posh people have of writing off a whole bunch of people. Anyone wearing sportswear and a baseball cap – Burberry back in the day – must be a petty criminal, on benefits, a dodgy sort. We all know the offensive words that should never be used to describe other people. To me, 'chav' is as bad as them.

I can't stand working-class people who use it either, trying to make out they're a bit better than their neighbours.

I come from that class of people, my mates were what others would have called chavs. They're as different as any other group of people. From the outside, they may look like a bunch of scrounging troublemakers but, let me tell you, there's plenty who would have had lots to offer, were they given the chance.

I am, in some ways, middle England's nightmare. I was a feral kid, a tagger with a spray can and felt tips, I had my first spliff before I was in double figures, lost my virginity when I was fourteen, had my first kid when unemployed, before I left my teens. I got one exam at school and I cheated on that.

My youth was spent on the streets of Custom House, drinking, playing football, arsing around. I was in regular trouble with the police – nicking, tagging, drugs, fighting. My parents had the police round the house regular and had to pick me up from the nick quite a few times.

Yet, really, I should represent middle England's hope. You see, the thing is, by luck, by the care of a great teacher and by the fact there was a drama school for underprivileged boys I could attend, I actually ended up making something of my life.

Some people might tell you, 'Everything I've ever got, I've got for myself.' Not so with me. It took people to invest time in me, energy and enthusiasm. It took a proper class teacher to encourage me to believe in myself.

I don't believe I'm unique, but I know that not everyone who was given the chance I had could take it. My upbringing has left me with the firm belief that a lot of kids from my background don't need clamping down on, locking up, ASBOs and all the rest of it. They need opportunity and to see that the opportunity exists from a young age.

I think a lot of people don't know what it's like to grow up in that background – where your friends all laugh at education, where gangs rule your life, where you're expected to be a criminal or a waster.

People view 'chavs' without any morals or feelings, as if they are animals. It's the old way of thinking they used to have with football. All football fans are hooligans, they are shit. This means we give them crumbling stadiums with toilets that would disgrace a war zone, herd them this way and that way, fence them in, call them scum.

You treat people like that, that's how they're gonna act. When the terrible events of Hillsborough brought things to a head, they realized you couldn't treat people like that no more. Now going to the football's like going to any other major event. There's no cages, the stadiums are all redone, people are treated with more respect and they act with more respect.

Take the riots a few years back. Some terrible things went on during them. You can't agree with it. So let me say directly, I didn't agree with the riots and felt very sorry for the people who died and lost property in them, as well as those who were traumatized and injured by them. It must have been terrifying. The riots were wrong and should never have happened.

However, it was dismissed as being 'non-political' – just the greedy hoodie generation taking the chance to go through the front of JD Sports. There's no doubt there were a few people like that. But you don't get so many people coming on to the streets unless there's a genuine sense of anger, combined with the idea that you have fuck all to lose.

I think it was a way of people having a voice. They was saying, 'You pen us into our little council estates, while you're sitting there you rich slags, laughing at us. So we're going to smash it all up, shit where we eat.' People feel they can't get attention in any other way. If you treat people like animals, they start acting like them. It wasn't down to Mark Duggan getting shot. It wasn't down to greed, either, like they tried to make out. Everyone had a fire in their belly. We just need to channel that fire towards politics and not towards violence. Then we can all change the world, I really believe that.

If you look at the reports on it, they showed that most of the rioters had fucked up their education, loads had been brought up in difficult circumstances, or had been chucked out of school. What stood out for me, seeing people interviewed on the telly, was how clear a lot of them were about having no chance. Get a load of this from *The Guardian*:

> While general levels of achievement for the group as a whole were relatively low, many were highly articulate and politicised, particularly when it came to describing the problems they faced, the frustrations in their lives, and the lack of opportunities available to them.

You know what that says to me? Absolutely fuck all, the first time I read it I didn't understand one word of it. Once I'd picked the bones out of it, though, it said that we have a load of potential there, a lot of clever people, who don't see anywhere to go but crime.

We have to reach them kids, don't we? I could easily have seen me getting swept up in all that when I was fourteen or fifteen, easily if it hadn't been for the acting. Why not? What had I got to look forward to? If you don't offer people a way forward, they will go backward.

Of course the chances of this government doing that are zero. It also makes me afraid for the future, too right.

It's the 'chavs' who get targeted for vandalism but it's the blokes in the suits that are the far worse culprits. They call it 'gentrification'. To me it's 'fuck you-ification'.

They're cutting the police, they're offering people no opportunity, handing whole areas over to drug dealers by making drugs illegal. Schools are facing cutbacks, social work, everything.

You've got a middle class that is trotting off on its gap years, indulging in a bit of social media

slacktivism about saving the fucking whale or whatever while an underclass is hemmed in by gang life
and lack of money so some of them can't leave their
own streets.

The trouble is that no one will speak out for these
people. They don't vote, not because they're too busy
sticking their arses to the sofa and sucking on Special
Brew but because they can't see anyone to vote for. So
if they ain't gonna vote, politicians ain't gonna pay
them any attention. The less attention they get, the less
likely they are to vote.

They go on about the rioters burning down buildings – rightly, that was disgusting. But the vandalism
developers have caused in traditional working-class
areas in London is much worse. Can a normal person
afford to live in the East End any more? Just about,
maybe, but once they've sold off the remaining council houses, and they've been sold for a fat profit to
developers or City workers, what will be left of the
communities? The Olympics fucked up more of my
area than rioters ever did.

You take the Clays Lane Housing Co-Op. Four
hundred and twenty-five people, men, women and
children evicted to build the athlete's village, and that
was far from the only bollocks that went on. How
much of the Olympic sponsorship money went to
compensating those people? Eight grand each, I heard,
for losing your home and community.

In Hackney, the council sold off Broadway Market to developers. Some of the businesses had been there thirty years and tried to buy the buildings themselves. No chance. They was sold to developers and now there's luxury flats there. Who benefits from that?

After the Olympics, house prices went up and councils like Newham started saying there was no social housing around – though there were plenty of empty houses. They shut down a young people's hostel and kicked out all the mothers and babies in it a couple of years ago.

The council also tried to flog off the Carpenters Estate to developers, though local people have managed to stop that happening so far.

I'm not going to pretend I knew all about these things before sitting down to write this, or that I've been involved in these campaigns for years. I haven't. I just know what I saw in my area, without particularly knowing the details. When I started to look into it, I found it was much worse than I thought.

It's the 'chavs' who get targeted for vandalism but it's the blokes in the suits that are the far worse culprits.

They call it 'gentrification'. To me it's 'fuck you-ification'.

Whose fault is this? Clearly the government's. They have to do something to stop it. The people who are poor in that area did nothing to deserve being poor. The rich people who are coming in are on benefits – the banks bailed out by mugs like you and me.

Having seen differences in wealth so close up, and having seen the destructive effects of money, and the lack of it, it seems clear to me that you have to offer people hope. Let me tell you this, if George Osborne had been born where I was, he would not be Chancellor of the Exchequer or whatever he is. He would have been just another mug on the dole, on drugs or in prison.

A working-class kid being born in the East End today has nothing like the chances of a kid just born to a normal middle-class family, let alone someone of the background of most of our politicians. And yet 'we're all in this together'? Yeah, right.

I think everyone has a talent of some sort but you are never going to exploit it unless you get the chance. I was massively lucky – not to get where I am, because I'm good at what I do and I worked hard for that – but to get the chance in the first place.

In the East End there might be people with the potential to be world-class scientists, doctors, anything. But you ain't never gonna be a violinist if you never have a violin, are you? And yet it's these people, not the rich people buying up their houses, meaning there's no council housing for the future, who have to bear the brunt of cuts.

It's a tragedy – and we need to do something about it.

29

Cockney rhyming slang is poetry, it's a code, it's a way of saying who we are.

The main thing people associate with Cockneys is rhyming slang, and I must confess, I do love a good rhyme.

Cockney rhyming slang is a wonderful thing – it's something that makes us unique around the world. In case you've been living under a rock, it's the East London way of speaking that replaces normal words with something that rhymes with them. Foreigners in particular seem to find it both fascinating and puzzling. I've had Americans ask me why, I'm not sure I know the answer. It's a laugh. Do you need a better reason?

Very often it'll be a phrase that replaces one word and you'll only use the first word of the phrase. This is the case in some of my favourites – haddock, as in 'haddock and bloater' for 'motor' i.e. 'car'. Kettle for watch. Kettle and hob, fob, get it? Not all the words have to rhyme. One I like at the moment is to call someone a 'slice' – i.e. they're not the full loaf. The new stuff is good too. 'I'll have a Nelson' – Nelson Mandela – Stella.

Some of the words have entered the language – 'get it into your loaf' means 'get it into your head' as in 'loaf of bread' meaning 'head'. There are lots of these: 'take a butcher's' – 'butcher's hook' means 'look'. People all over the country know what these things mean.

No one else quite has that, it's poetry, it's a code, it's a way of saying who we are.

Not all Cockneys use it, by any means. Some find it a bit embarrassing.

A lot, though, are really proud of it. My dad loves his slang. I remember watching a Bob Monkhouse show once and they had a question: 'What does battle cruiser mean in Cockney rhyming slang?' The answer was 'boozer'. My dad hit the roof. I've never seen him so angry in my life. He was shouting at the TV, 'Bollocks! I've been round pubs in the East End all my life and I ain't never heard anything like that!'

It means an awful lot to some people. A lot of people think that Cockney is a term for any Londoner but it actually means someone who was born within the sound of Bow Bells. That's Bow Bells of St Mary-Le-Bow in the City of London, which ain't even in what you think of as the East End. They reckon back in the day you could hear the bells six miles to the east, four miles to the west, five miles to the north and three to the south. Most people when they hear the word think of the East End, though. The legend says that Dick Whittington – the geezer with the moody cat – was at Highgate when he heard the bells calling him back, telling him he'd be three times Lord Mayor of London. He must have been right off his nut.

It started me thinking about what the history of the whole thing is. How do we come to speak in this funny, sing-song way? I was really surprised to find out that the word Cockney trod pretty much the same route as 'chav'. It used to mean a small, weedy boy back in the Middle Ages – Cockenay – which sounds like Matt Lucas taking the piss. Then it ended up being a word used to slag off people who lived in town and eventually the working class of the East End. Chav used to mean 'kid' as well and was eventually used to slag off working-class people.

The East End was always a big immigrant area and the language borrowed a fair bit from Romany – words like 'kushty' for good and 'wonga' for money – and also from Yiddish – 'kosher' and 'schtum', as in 'keep schtum'.

Apparently Cockney rhyming slang might be what was once known as a 'thieves' cant'. This is a language villains could use among themselves so the Old Bill didn't know what they was talking about.

From the minute people started to talk about the East End – back in Victoria's day – it's been seen as a den of wheeler dealers. Apparently, if you said you was an East Ender people would get bug powder out to sprinkle you with, serious. There was the idea of the 'respectable poor' and we wasn't them.

What they didn't realize was that people were dirty because they was poor. When they set up a bath-house for people to wash in, it got over-run.

There's a bit of an echo of that moody vibe in how people see Cockneys today – I saw an article saying the accent would inspire the least confidence in passengers if it was used by an airline pilot. I don't see why. I should have thought it sounded friendly. 'Awright, my darlin's, strap yaselves dahn, in a coupla ticks the geeza in the plane in front will fuck off and we'll be well ready to do one lively. Don't forget to adjust ya kettles to an hour in front fa local time. Propa nawty!' I don't see why not.

Get in the haddock, you slice!

Cockneys have always been ones to tell authority where to go – so maybe the voice ain't associated with being in command.

We've got on the tits of polite society for years and years. When people think of East London they inevitably think of the Pearlies – known to outsiders as Pearly Kings and Queens. Now, it might surprise you to learn that not everyone in London dresses like that

24/7. Nor do we run down the street clicking our heels and saying, 'Gawd bless ya, Guv'nor,' like in *Oliver!* Well, not unless we're paid to – if they ever remake the film, they've got my number.

The Pearlies do show that Cockneys have always stood up for themselves and stuck together. They're descended from the 'Coster Kings' – strong working-class men elected to be the representative of each borough. They were like trade unions of their day. The women of the markets were meant to be fierce too – particularly Billingsgate fish market. This is where the expression 'fishwife' comes from, I should think – tough ladies with gobs on 'em like the Blackwall Tunnel.

Like I said, the area's always been associated with being radical. We've had riots and strikes here for as long as anyone can remember. The feminist movement kicked off here too – the old Suffragette birds. One of 'em, Sylvia Pankhurst, ran a cost-price kitchen for the poor and held rallies for women's rights. It seems a lot of the people supported her.

You might think that the nutty way of speaking came out of all this, a little bit of light relief.

Back in the day – for nearly 1,000 years – London used to have people called costermongers. These was market traders and, by Queen Victoria's time, they had their own chat, called Coster back slang, which was like a forerunner of rhyming slang. They made words up, turned 'em round and give 'em a jumble. They used it to confuse punters and the Old Bill. There's an amazing book called *Shadows of the Workhouse* by Jennifer Worth, all about London in the Victorian era. Cop a loada this, it sounds like something out of *Clockwork Orange*:

'Jack, 'e 'ad a regular tosseno tol. 'Ad a showful. Bigger loof 'im.' (Jack had bad luck. Had bad money. More fool him.)

And how about:

'Sey, I done a doogheno flash, today. But kool 'im. Who's he?' (Say, I done a good deal today. Look at him. Who's he?)

Mad, eh?

These costermongers got right up the hooters of the gentry. They knew they was doing it too and set out to annoy 'em!

Like a lot of lower-class people, they loved a bit of bling. So they started sewing mother-of-pearl buttons, on the knackered clothes they wore. Part of it was to take the piss out of the West End lot with all their fancy clothes.

They was anti-authority, not out of spite but because authority had never done nothing for them. Who does that sound like? This lot had to stick together – their shouting and bad language (don't blame me, it's in me blood) annoyed the posh people and they was always complaining about them. No one was gonna help 'em. They had to help themselves.

So eventually a friend of the costermongers – a rat catcher and road sweeper called Henry Croft – decorated his whole suit with shiny buttons to raise money for charity. The costermongers used to look after their own and, in the days before the NHS, had a hospital fund.

The thing about these people is they didn't have any money but still they looked out for everyone else. They had to – the posh people weren't going to give 'em the shit off their shoes. Some of 'em couldn't go out if it was raining. They only had one set of clothes, and if they got soaked, they could freeze to death in their houses – no heating for them – or catch a chill that would put 'em out of action for a long period. That meant starvation or being carted off to a workhouse.

It was like a ghetto in East London back then – costermongers sold to the poor because proper shops were too expensive or wouldn't let working-class people in.

The costermongers were always harassed by the Old Bill. They wasn't even allowed to stand still to make a sale, well, if the Old Bill caught 'em. So they had to keep pushing their barrows – these were the famous barrow boys.

I'm proud to have come out of this tradition and I feel a lot of warmth towards them people. I think that's great, when the world's against you, to all stand together and look out for each other. I like what I read about 'em too. They were right pissheads, apparently, when they got the chance, loved 'avin' it.

I sometimes wonder if we're heading back to them days, when there was no state help, no healthcare if you couldn't pay for it. You think I'm over the top on that? Well, we'll wait and see, won't we?

They say rhyming slang will disappear in thirty years' time, to be replaced by Jafaican – the new Ali G-style way of speaking. Maybe it will in East London. But a lot of the people moved out to Essex, which is where a lot of the accent came from in the first place, they say. Perhaps it'll live on there. I hope so.

30

I can't stand bullies, never have been able to, and Jeremy Kyle is a classic bully, picking on people who haven't had his chances in life or education just to feel better than them.

I have just found out the most depressing fact I think I've heard for years. All right, it's not poverty, it's not war, it's not none of them things. But it is bad. How bad? Dry rot in the attic? Worse, by far. Don't even come close. Rot my attic until the beams crumble, but don't give me this. Daughter going out with a boy band backing singer? Worse again. I would rather my daughter went out with the lowest, do-nothing, lip-syncing, stool-sitting waste of fake tan on the planet than this. OK, ready. Sit down. Take the weight off ya plates, you don't want to be standing when this hits ya.

Jeremy Kyle supports West Ham. Drink that in. Look, there's a golden rule in life. West Ham don't allow wankers. That's it. If you're a wanker, there are plenty of clubs for you – I don't have to name 'em.

But Jeremy Kyle! I used to goad mates of mine who are Chelsea about David Mellor or Man U about

Harry Styles. For fuck sake Man United have got Miley Cyrus! Now I can't hold my head up. I've got nothing to say. It's like every other team has this massive trump card they can play against us.

I'm proper shaken.

I despise Jeremy Kyle, every bone in his stuck-up, sanctimonious, two-faced body. He's a former addicted gambler whose ex-wife claims that he took thousands from her. He licks his mobile phone for comfort. That's what he says in his autobiography.

Also, try this quote from him, from the *Birmingham Mail*. Jeremy says:

> The reason I lick my [golf] balls in this way is probably more strange than the licking of the balls themselves. It's just that cleaning my balls on the pristine, white towel dangling from my golf bag might in turn make my golf towel dirty. And I most certainly could not have that, I really couldn't!

I'm not making this up. It's like Alan Partridge, only with a vicious twist.

If you don't know *The Jeremy Kyle Show*, lucky you. He gets people on pretending to help work out their problems but just goads them and mocks them in front of an invited studio audience.

He's a smug exploiter of misery, a nasty piece of work. To me, he's a Judas, smiling to people's faces, luring them on his show and then turning on them for 'entertainment'. This slag had the front to call his book *I'm Only Being Honest*. He don't know the meaning of the word.

We don't have to go far to understand what's behind all this. Jeremy is just another posh boy laughing at ordinary people. His dad was personal secretary to the Queen Mother. So how much feeling do you think he really has for them he exploits? How much understanding can he have of the problems they face? He was born with a silver spoon in his mouth.

Look, there's a golden rule in life. West Ham don't allow wankers. That's it. If you're a wanker, there are plenty of clubs for you – I don't have to name 'em.

Also, I wonder – and I've no way of backing this up, it's just a thought – if part of his confessed mental problems come from guilt, not living up to the standards his dad set. His dad was chatting to the Queen Mum on a daily basis, not taking money to torment some smack addict from Portsmouth like a weird pimp.

I can't stand bullies, never have been able to, and Jeremy Kyle is a classic bully, picking on people who haven't had his chances in life or education just to feel better than them. The show should be ditched, tomorrow.

I'm not the only one who thinks he should be taken off air.

A few years ago, one of the geezers on the show headbutted a lodger who had shagged his missus. He finished up in front of a judge who said the show's producers should have been in the dock beside him.

Now remember, this judge deals with all sorts of villainy every day. He sees the very worst of people. Murder, robbery, worse. So what do you think it takes to knock his syrup sideways? Something out of the ordinary range of human nastiness. Hello, it's Jeremy Kyle! He called Kyle out on saying the show helps people too. He said they were self-righteous and basically full of bullshit.

It's interesting to find out how that show operates. Have a Google, you won't believe what these slags get up to to get people to tear into each other.

If anyone says, 'Have you paid your missus back yet?' or 'Have a lick of ya phone, ya mug!' I expect they cut that out too. I'm not knocking people with obsessive compulsive disorder, by the way. It's a serious condition that needs understanding. I am mocking a slag, giving him the treatment he hands out to others. It's strange he's got OCD, though, because in any photo I've ever seen of him, his cuffs never look quite level. If you're reading this, Jeremy, you might want to check that a few thousand times.

Kyle picks vulnerable people, drug addicts, alcoholics, people suffering from divorce, people adjusting to life after being inside and preys on them. This is the work of a cunt. He even looks knocky to me. He used to be a salesman, apparently. I wouldn't buy nothing off the melt.

He uses all the tricks to try to start a tear-up. One bloke, Terry Carvell, claims Kyle rammed the microphone into his chin, trying to get him to hit him.

There are real psychologists involved in this. I don't know how they can justify it to themselves. All that bollocks about aftercare – people who have been on the show will tell you different. Isn't there a professional body of psychologists who can look into this and ask if their members should be involved in it? It makes me think a lot worse of any profession that will allow its members to take part in this circus. I would say it's disreputable, but that's just my opinion. It would take a proper professional body to rule on that.

They use lie detectors too – a machine any psychologist will tell you doesn't work. You'd be more effective chucking someone in a bag, throwing 'em in the river and seeing if they float, like they used to do with the old witches. Do none of the psychologists involved in the show think they should point this out?

Then there's *Jeremy Kyle's Emergency Room* – a show that has prompted critics to ask, 'Can TV go any lower?' I'm sure it can, as we'll find out when we see what Jeremy does next.

I'd like to address Jeremy here directly, just to issue a plea to him. Jeremy, you shouldn't be a West Ham fan. You're from Reading. Support Reading, they're a perfectly good club. They may even have facilities to deal with wankers. We at West Ham haven't. There aren't any specific 'wanker units' in the ground, no twat access or dickhead suites. So, right from the bottom of my heart, Jeremy, if there's any spark of humanity left in you, any at all, keep away from Upton Park, drop the West Ham support and, most of all, sincerely, fuck right off, forever. Sorry if that upsets you but I'm only being honest.

31

Art is something that gets you by the bollocks.

What is art? A lot of people ask this question and I'm happy to be able to clear it up once and for all. Art is something that gets you by the bollocks.

I'm glad to have sorted that out for ya. It's a work of human creation that moves you inside. I would say it has to inspire, to terrify, to soothe, to hypnotize. A lot of stuff I've seen recently goes on shock value. There's nothing wrong with that but it's got a bit boring now. It's not shocking to be shocked any more.

My favourite modern artist is Piet Mondrian. I love the way he handles colour, the formality of the lines combine with the surprise of the irregular placing of colour and ... ah, did I have you going there? I just Googled the melt. Never heard of him, to be honest.

I'm in two minds about modern art. On the one hand, it's clearly a heap of crap – in some cases, quite literally. If you Google 'body fluids in modern art' you'll see they've done a table for all these artists, depending on what they use. You've got little tick boxes – vomit, semen, blood, urine, faeces and 'other'. What happened to 'paint'?

There's a geezer called Andres Serrano who's got five out of six but I reckon there's a gap in the market there for someone to come up with the full six. They could make millions.

Tracey Emin's *My Bed* was interesting. I saw that and could only think that it looked quite tidy after a weekend at it. I nearly rung her up to ask for her cleaner's number.

Damien Hirst's stuff is all right, I suppose. Fish in a tank, long title, bish bosh bash, millions of quid. Gotta love that.

I do respect modern artists in that way, like you might respect a daring bank robber. It's a bit of the old Punk thing, which I know about because I played Sid Vicious in a play. I could imagine Damien at the end of his life turning round to the art critics and saying, 'Ever felt you've been cheated?' like the Sex Pistols did on their final gig. Go on, son, you blag all the cash you can!

Grayson Perry's another – very funny bloke, love him as a person. His art, a bit like what you find out the back of a school art room after the remedial class has been in. Cocks on pots, Grayson. We all did that back in the day – I made a whole row of 'em out of clay in the art room once. I didn't expect an exhibition at the Tate for 'em.

So I love that about the modern artists – ordinary kids from ordinary backgrounds putting the swindle on the stuck-up idiots of the art world. Proper naughty. There, you know you were dying for me to say it the whole book. I'll say it again. Proper naughty.

What I love about modern art is this: there's no skill to it. They say it's all about an idea, but any twat can have an idea. Ideas are the easy bit. I've had an idea for a flying car. It's great. No wings, doesn't need petrol, drives you home if you've had one too many. The difficult bit is making it.

I've also had the idea of taking on five defenders, rounding the keeper and backheeling it into the net in the last minute of a West Ham–

A thing I don't get about modern art is this: why do they need a little sticker on the side of it, telling you what it's about?

Tottenham cup final. That's OK then, that's the same as doing it, ain't it.

I'm a sort of artist myself – that's what an actor is. You'd think I work only with ideas, and that what comes out of my mouth is all planned. But it don't always work like that. There's always an element of improvised performance, you being up against the limitations of the set, your own talent, the other actors, sometimes the audience, that makes the performance more than what you had in your nut.

If you're claiming that your idea has been completely taken out of your nut by whoever the poor melt is you get to design and make it, you have to be wrong, don't you? That artist is doing what you should be doing, working with the material, getting the feedback from the stuff, changing and improvising.

Sometimes you don't even really have an idea of what's going to happen as an actor, you just live it. It's not something that's coming out the inside of you, it's coming from somewhere else – the words of the writer, the atmosphere, the feedback of other actors. If everything ended up on the screen exactly as I'd thought about it, it would be pretty dull for me.

Harold Pinter used to go on about this. He'd say characters would appear to him from nowhere. One second he had no idea of them, the next they were speaking to him on the page. He said that then he had to work with them, knock them into shape, argue with them even. He didn't just turn to an assistant and go, 'I tell you what, I've had this idea for a character. He's called Joey. Boxer. Works in demolition. Here, Dave, you do the rest, after you've got us a coffee from round the corner.'

Ideas are all very well but the best music, art, acting, writing, whatever, says something a lot more than can be summed up in an idea. If it can be summed up easily then it ain't really art.

A thing I don't get about modern art is this: why do they need a little sticker on the side of it, telling you what it's about? When I was working with Harold, he never explained anything, wouldn't explain it. If he could have said it differently, he wouldn't have needed to write the play, would he? He'd have just stuck a sticker in a theatre saying what he's interested in. These stickers always say, 'What interests the artist is blah, blah.' Well, what interests me is West Ham, a quiet life and what's coming up next on *Antiques Roadshow*. When you watch me on *EastEnders*, you don't need a little sticker on the side of the telly telling you that, though, do you?

And have you ever seen a video installation? What the fuck are they about? They could be called 'How not to make a film'. Look, video installation artists, give Nick Love a bell or anyone on *EastEnders* and they'll tell you how to make something that's a little bit more interesting than one of my old man's home videos. I saw one that had a bird with a box on her head and a lamp coming out of it. If you want that, I'm sure I could find you a couple of old acid heads who'd come up with something twice as weird for half the price.

If you ever go in an art gallery, it's worth watching how people react to these video installations. They glance at them, there's no real reaction. They might sit for a bit but I've never seen anyone get all the way through one.

32

*If the political parties had to raise their own fund-
ing from ordinary people they'd be lucky to get a bit
of chewing gum and three 1970s Pesetas in their
collecting tins.*

I am never likely to be Prime Minister. For a start I
don't like lying and I didn't go to the right school. But
this is a question I got asked once and it did set me
thinking.

I never thought a lot about politics. I just about
remember the Thatcher years, not too well, but I
know there was a lot of hate towards her. I don't
know exactly why. All I remember is my old man
going on about how selfish they were and how they
were all in it for themselves. Round where I grew up,
it's all about looking after yourself, people don't have
a lot of time for political organizations or anything
like that.

Having said that, that wasn't always the way in the
East End – the docks weren't afraid to strike and Keir
Hardie, one of the first socialist MPs, was MP for West
Ham South.

Back in the 1930s the fascist twat Oswald Mosley tried to march through the East End with his Blackshirts and the police turned out in force to support him to make sure he got through. Well, if you want to have it, this has always been the place to come.

He was met by the Claret and Blue of West Ham, as the whole manor turned out to fight him, and he had plenty of claret on him by the time the day was over. Mind you, blood was the least of his worries. Apparently, women were flinging pots of shit from windows at him and the police who were trying to protect him. The Blackshirts got ironed out, proper.

Doing the research for this book, I was fascinated to come across these stories from Hammers fans of old who had similar tales of solidarity against the Blackshirts. On the Knees Up Mother Brown website, a fan called MARC remembers a day in 1936 when football was put to one side and West Ham fans stood 'shoulder to shoulder with Trade Unionists, Jewish and Irish groups, Anarchists and Communists', brought together by their mutual desire to stop the British Union of Fascists marching through the area.

Here's another, which proves the age-old saying, 'Before fucking with someone, make sure you know with who it is you fuck.' Or is it 'whom'? Never got that.

Another fan, Georgee Paris, remembers the story that his nan used to tell about her childhood. She used to hang out at her friend's sweet shop on Cable Street, and one time the Blackshirts smashed the shop window – because they were Jewish. They had to hole up in a back room of the shop until his nan's dad, who was a docker, arrived with a gun. Georgee said his nan 'was always very proud of the East Enders chucking out the Blackshirts'.

All that was deep history by the time I was growing up and I only heard about it much later. Does it shape you? Maybe – some things are just in the water, ain't they? Maybe the ghosts of those West Ham fans and feisty dockers still stroll around the manor today. I don't know, I've never really had a political thought in my head until I came to write this.

The first thing I'd do if I was Prime Minister, though, is put some normal people in the government. At the moment most of the people in the Cabinet and all the people at the top seem to be private-school educated or out of Oxford or Cambridge. They're not everyday people.

I ain't got nothing against private schools – I send my kids to one. It seems to me, though, that they're vastly over-represented in the corridors of power. A lot of the bollocks that goes on wouldn't happen if working-class people were given more of a say. There's no way we would allow them to chop up the NHS or do all this bedroom tax or whatever.

Yes, you can argue, 'They've got the same chance as every other mug of being elected,' but that don't paint the full picture. Standing as a candidate for Parliament is a full-time job and it don't pay. What normal person has got the funds to take two years out or whatever to get elected? It's a carve-up and there should be some way of getting people who've actually lived some life into government, rather than this present lot who are just groomed for power from an early age.

When I looked at the parties in the last election, I couldn't see anyone like me. There are no working-class people in politics, not that sound working class. Well, maybe one or two – I can think of Dennis Skinner – but anyone who gets anywhere close to leading the parties sounds like the Duke of Edinburgh to me.

David Cameron. He's a man who looks like he's wearing one of them cardboard masks of himself. I have nothing in common with the fella. How is he supposed to stand up for normal people? The other two, Clegg and Miliband were the same. I like Diane Abbott because she's from a working-class back-ground but even she thinks she has to sound posh, I don't know why.

Maybe she thinks many people in this country still have a thing inside their head that makes them respect a posh voice, no matter what it's saying. But I reckon most working-class people turn off the TV as soon as the jelly moulds appear. You can't tell one from another. It's like *Attack of the Clones*.

The political system is there for the taking, for a working-class party, that talk like working-class people and stand up for the interests of working-class people, not trying to divide people by banging on about immigration and all that.

I feel I've got more in common with some bloke from Albania who's come over here tying himself to the bottom of the train than I have with anyone leading the political parties. The whole thing's a carve-up. There's no real politics any more, just a bunch of oily melts from the same background crawling their way up a greasy pole for personal gain.

I think these parties would disappear if they didn't get propped up by huge payments from various dodgy individuals in the super rich. If they had to raise their own funding from ordinary people they'd be lucky to get a bit of chewing gum and three 1970s Pesetas in their collecting tins. I've got no time for any of them.

It's a monopoly – small parties can't get any representation in the press, can't compete with donations from people who are buying up our politics by the yard. The Tories' and Labour's time is past, the Liberals has never been as far as I know. We need something new.

So who would I have in my Cabinet? Who's in the team to propel us to a new and exciting future?

My fiancée Jo would be my first appointment. I see her in a sort of enforcer role. If the Prime Minister's message ain't getting across to the other people in the government, she'll go over and kick it into 'em. She's had to bring up the family on next to no money sometimes and put up with nasty surprises – like the time we found out my bar bill for the year at the Groucho Club was £30,000. She helped me deal with that, identified the problem (me), addressed it (in no uncertain terms) and moved on. I still bear the scars. I reckon she'd be like 'minister without portfolio but with big stick', a sort of Malcolm Tucker figure from *The Thick of It*, only Cockney and a bit more sweary and scary. She can be a bit indecisive, Jo, but I think that'd make her more difficult to deal with for people who stepped out of line. Keep 'em guessing.

I like Russell Brand and think he speaks a lot of sense. He's a West Ham fan so I suppose that disposes me to think well of him. He's also been very good to me. When I started *EastEnders*, Russell found out my number, texted me and just said a couple of beautiful little lines of advice about how best to cope with the new level of fame. He didn't have to do that at all, he don't know me, but he did and I respected him for that. Maybe one day we'll meet and talk.

He takes a lot of shit and people seem to think he's some sort of communist radical but really the things he says are just obvious to anyone of a certain background. To me half of the stuff he comes out with doesn't even sound debatable, it's just straightforward fact.

All right, sometimes he don't do himself any favours but his heart's in the right place – he cares for people, genuinely, even if sometimes he says it in a way that's easy to misunderstand.

You can laugh at all that 'love' stuff he says but what else is there, when it comes down to it? I'm not half as clever as him and prefer a crumpet pissing with Marmite of an evening to eating a dictionary but there are some things that seem so basic that surely we can all agree on them.

I recommend actually watching Russell's podcasts and thinking about what he says and making up your own mind about it.

Other people I'd stick in the government include Johnny Vegas. I love Johnny, he's straightforward, honest and very kind. He'd be my Chancellor and ensure we got re-elected year after year because there's no way he'd be upping the tax on booze and fags. He'd also bung some cash at the students – I know he thinks going to art school was massive for him. I don't know what the fuck they taught him, because I've seen his pottery and it looks like he was pissed when he made it, which to be fair he probably was. I think it's important that people without a trust fund get a right to an education. The arts take a right bashing off people but they contribute about

£80 billion a year to the economy, which is a lot of money for something that's meant to be a waste of time. I wish I'd had something a bit sooner that taught me to think. You need education for more than just propping up society, you need to feed people the ideas to change it.

I'd have Maddy Hill who plays my on-screen daughter in there too. She's a brilliant actress who is going to go a long way, believe me. She's a girl out the flats in Hackney, down to earth and with a lot to say about the world – as you can see if you follow her on Twitter. She's very into this affordable housing for young people thing, which I think is really important. I've got no idea how people on a normal wage are supposed to earn enough to get their own house nowadays. She's always supporting some campaign or another – she does one for ending child marriage and another for ending poverty. I know she lived for under a quid a day for a while. She's also not afraid to keep me in line and describes me as 'a

Paul Gascoigne's someone I look up to, too, but I don't think we'd be having him in the Cabinet. Maybe in the Lords, where his drink problem wouldn't stand out so much.

preposterous human being'. Sounds about right. It's a pleasure to work with her.

Julie Walters is another diamond. I'd have her in there tomorrow. One of the proudest moments of my life was when I saw she'd said she had started watching *EastEnders* again and she loved the character of Mick Carter. That woman is a legend. What hasn't she done in acting? I didn't even know she knew who I was! A real thrill for me but that's not the reason I'd have her in the government. From what I've read of her politics, she feels as let down by politicians as I do and thinks it's time for something new. She's talked about how difficult it is for working-class actors today. I think this is true. A lot of the time you have middle-class drama about middle-class people. That's partly because the TV companies have all got their eyes on the international market and, to your average American, everyone in the UK talks like Jeremy Irons. People like me need subtitles out there.

The reason Julie brings such a big amount of heart to her roles is that she's lived a life outside acting. It wasn't just posh school, RADA then Shakespeare, with no idea what everyday life was like. She was a nurse first. I think that's incredible too – actually starting in acting so late. You need to be a really blinding talent to do that.

The other thing I admire about her is how many different parts she's done. She's not limited to comedy or drama. I would love to follow in her footsteps one day – it must be great to be able to do a sketch show, a Hollywood film and a TV drama. Did you see her play that old TV moaner Mary Whitehouse? It was incredible. There was a woman who, as far as I could see, would be as welcome as subsidence next door to you. But she made you like her, even root for her. Amazing.

She describes herself as having been 'angry at everything'. I can dig that. I feel like that myself sometimes. As an actor you're always looking inward, worried about your next job or, if you're being successful, having people always asking you about yourself. It takes a lot to stay focused on the things that really matter in life.

In interviews Julie sounds as pissed off as me with the state of politics and said she couldn't find anyone to vote for. On that alone, I say, 'Get in the Cabinet, babes.' I'd probably make her Secretary of State for Treacles, as I think she would make a good voice for women.

Micky Flanagan would have to be in there somewhere. He was a fish porter at Billingsgate and knows what's what. It's amazing how Cockneys still have the Alf Garnett stereotype, but that's far from the truth. Micky's a compassionate geezer who would do well for the country. He's a proper Londoner, a Cockney and has that 'fuck you' way about him, says it how it is – his views on life are shaped by his experiences. I know he don't go on about politics much in his act because he appreciates people come for a laugh, not a lecture. But he's got no bullshit about him and that's an important thing in a government.

I'd have Danny Baker in there too, though he's a Millwall fan so I'd have to keep an eye on him. You couldn't make him Defence Secretary or he'd be singing 'No One Likes Us' at the French. You couldn't send him to an international meeting because he'd be chanting 'you'll never make the Eurotunnel' at the other ministers. That's just what Millwall are like. All of 'em. Even the babies. Danny's good with words so he could be the press spokesman. Unlike most of the people here, he's used to not swearing so he'd be best for the job.

I love Paul O'Grady and I'd make him Minister of Justice, because then I reckon we'd finally get to the bottom of this Hillsborough thing, see a few bankers locked up, and send a few of these well-connected nonces where they belong.

Paul's brilliant because, like the others, he's funny and he isn't afraid to take the piss out of himself. That's what seems missing in modern politicians – they take themselves too seriously, are all about their image. They're afraid of coming over like human beings.

I'd have Bill Hicks in the Cabinet too. I know he's dead and American but he'd still make a better contribution than most. That's a conspiracy for me. He died far too early, a sudden death. Did he have too much to say? Did he annoy the wrong people? This wasn't a quiet man, this was a style of comedy that was really challenging to the powers that be.

There's no one doing that kind of stuff really in this country at the moment. We're living in the world of Michael McIntyre, not a funny bone in his body. No disrespect, he's cracking on and good luck to him but I'd rather have a bit of Chubby Brown. At least he stands out from the wallpaper.

I'd stick Noel Gallagher in there too. He's a bloke who says what he thinks and who thinks a lot. I've met Noel a few times and I really like him. I was at the NME awards and I saw him just as I was leaving. I'm not someone who gets starstruck, but I had to go up and say hello to him. As I approached him, he stuck out his hand and said, 'Hello Dan.' I couldn't believe he knew who I was, and more than that he'd been following my career. He said, 'I think you're a great actor but you're a bit typecast.' I like that about him, he's not crawling up my arse, just saying what he thinks. He said that if I was in a band, I'd be the band of the people. I couldn't believe this, it was like a dream.

As we were leaving the security assumed that we were together and ushered me into his limo after him. I got in and sat down and he said, 'What are you doing?' I felt such a melt. I said, 'Here, just do us a favour and drop us around the corner so I don't look like a complete twat.' He said, 'What are you on about? I'm going to Kasabian's after party, come with me.' He said Tom, the lead singer, was a massive fan of mine and we would surprise him. Wow! I was still trying to be cool round him but I'm not sure I was doing a very good job at that point. I wanted to ask a million questions but I played it down because I thought he was looking at me like we were on the same level. In his eyes maybe we were, in mine we weren't. He's Noel Gallagher. A legend.

We swapped digits at the end of it all, but I never had the arsehole to ring the number.

I don't often brown-nose people but I am going to say this, because it's true. I was so grateful to Noel Gallagher in the nineties. I was an acid house kiddie and I loved all that – what my dad calls boom boom music. It was a time of expression and a whole cultural movement. All my pals had decks round their houses, mixing and scratching and I used to love them days, sitting round their bedrooms puffing away, listening to them on the decks. You couldn't hear each other talk, it was so loud. But, let's be honest, you had to be off your nut to appreciate the music. Without the drugs it was rubbish. It was Oasis that brought us out of that and I'm forever thankful. It was brilliant to go to a gig and listen to a proper band playing proper music instead of something that's been made on a computer.

I've got 50 Cent's number after we did a film together but I never called that either. He said he thought I was like the English Robert De Niro but I've never felt that cool. I wouldn't have 50 Cent in the Cabinet, though, he's too focused on his own career. We'd stock his mineral water for him if he fancied it, though, get through a few bottles of that.

Paul Gascoigne's someone I look up to, too, but I don't think we'd be having him in the Cabinet. Maybe in the Lords, where his drink problem wouldn't stand out so much.

Paul was a genius and a maverick. I love the fact that he just said what he wanted to say, he didn't care what people thought of him. But when he got on the football pitch no one could touch him. Well-behaved players couldn't do what he did. It's scary to think what he's resorted to.

Without that talent, he was always going off the rails. I think if he hadn't found that footballing talent he would have been banged up or become an alcoholic a lot sooner. It's just when his talent could no longer serve him, there was nowhere else left for him to go.

I met him a couple of times and now he looks like a skeleton. If you threw a ball at him now, he couldn't trap a ball. It's horrible. He's sucking on the bottle, or the bottle's sucking on him every time he puts it to his lips. It's an illness, a disease. We'll look back at him and we'll be saying, 'Why didn't we help him?' Well, some people have tried that, but at the end of the day it's down to him. What can you do? Anyway, he seems like an ideal candidate for the upper house. A bit of a lightweight for some of them maybe but I reckon he'd look good in a syrup. Do they still wear syrups?

I'd have doctors and nurses and midwives in the Cabinet, people like that who have worked because they want to help people. It's not about money or anything like that for them. To me, they have an aura about them.

I'd also like my brother in there. He's the strongest person I know. When he was a kid he was much more interested in playing with girls than boys. He used to like skipping. You can imagine how that went down on the manor. He didn't give a fuck. He wanted to skip, he was going to skip. I was weaker, I used to suck up to the hard kids because life was easier that way. He'd defy them. I used to try to get to him, say, 'Come and play football,' but he wouldn't have it.

When I think about it now he was braver than everyone in that school because he went against the grain. He had the arsehole to do that. To do that at an East London school takes bollocks.

Somehow he managed to get a good load of exams an' all. He's married now and mad into cooking and stuff like that. He still has the same best friend as he had when he was a kid – a girl – and they all go on holiday together, him, his wife, her and her husband.

My brother amazes me. We went round his house the other day and he served us pesto with pasta. He had made pesto himself! Can you imagine that? Actually made it, when you can easily buy it in a shop. His ideal present, which we got him for his birthday, was a little pamphlet, with recipes for meals from all around the world on it. Your one from Africa, one from Thailand that kind of thing. I went round there the other night and everything is prepped, all ready to go in Tupperware boxes. He was showing off a new wok he had. I was sitting there watching him and I was thinking, 'I'd love to have a bit of that about me.' He thinks I should start cooking. I do good spaghetti Bolognese but that's about it. I suppose really it's only opening the jar, not real cooking. He says cooking is therapeutic. I suppose there's something to that – it makes quite a satisfying 'pop' when you break the lid on a jar of tomato sauce.

He's a very cultured boy. How does that happen? I wouldn't say that he was in any shape or form a product of his environment. It's a mystery how you turn out like him, given the upbringing he had. Where would he be if he'd had more of a chance? I reckon he could have done anything. Yeah, I'd put my brother in my Cabinet, purely for his walnut and cheese bread.

He'd be my Minister of Culture, largely because out of all the people here, I reckon he knows the most about it.

33

If we want austerity, let's start with the MPs.

So we've got the Cabinet sorted, what policies are we going to put in?

I think every human being should be able to eat and to have access to water. End of. You shouldn't have to march three miles to get water for your kids. How is it that over here we drink bottled water but there are parts of the world where they can't even have a well?

We walk around moaning about the milk going off while billions of people can't eat. We should share the money out and share the wealth out so every human being can have a decent life.

I'm not trying to come over as a saint because, God knows, I like my plasma screen TV and my nice motor as much as anyone, and nowadays I get paid all right – though most of my life I haven't had a pot to piss in. But surely there is enough money around so that everyone in the world can have enough food for their kids.

I am patriotic and very proud to be British. I was brought up on stories of the war and how my area suffered under the Blitz, standing up to Hitler. But I don't think our responsibilities as human beings end at these shores, particularly when we have caused a load of problems in the first place. You can't go into a country, bomb the living shit out of it and then say, 'Sorry not our problem.' These wars – though I've got massive respect for the soldiers who fight them, I certainly couldn't do it – were an expensive mistake, most importantly in terms of lives but also in the cost to the country.

When I pay my taxes I'd rather it go on a decent hospital for my nan than on a bomb to blow up some poor mug on the other side of the earth because Tony Blair says he thinks he might be about to do the same to us with 'weapons of mass destruction'.

So why ain't we doing the same to North Korea who admit to having weapons of mass destruction? Let's put it this way, Kim Jong-un must be shitting himself in case oil gets discovered under him.

Tony Blair. What a rat. I'd have an investigation into that melt as quick as you like. Did he lie to us about Iraq? My money's on 'yes'. He's a bloke who used being Prime Minister as a career move and now goes around the world on a private jet blowing smoke up the arses of oligarchs and absolutely minting it. How did he ever claim to understand normal people? If he did he'd never show his face in public again.

Harold Pinter used to talk about him and say he was a war criminal who should be tried for his crimes. If Harold says he's a war criminal, he's a war criminal in my book.

In Harold's acceptance speech when he got his Nobel Prize, he said:

How many people do you have to kill before you qualify to be described as a mass murderer and a war criminal? One hundred thousand? More than enough, I would have thought.

If we want austerity, let's start with the MPs. They should get paid an average wage plus overtime. No consultancies, no backhanders, nothing. Then maybe some of these posh mugs would drop out and leave governing the country to people who had to live in the real world and were doing the job for reasons other than getting invited onto some oligarch's yacht.

They say they wouldn't get anyone decent to do it for that money. Bollocks. Nurses work for a lot less and I'd put my trust in their common sense before I would this lot who've never had to worry about paying a bill in their life. Making MPs take an average wage would mean their interests were the same as the people they were representing. The country would be run for the people, not business. You can't get people with the right attitude into Parliament while you're paying them so much money. They've nothing in common with most of the country and the high wage attracts money-grabbing psychos.

Before you say, 'How can you say that when you're on a wedge?' – I ain't representing anyone. I've also known what it is to be skint for most of my life.

Everyone seems to be in with the swindle except the working-class people. But it's the working-class people who have got the power to change it.

I'd cut some foreign aid too, well the foreign aid we send to the USA, where we very kindly agree to chip into their nuclear programme to the tune of billions for exactly no control whatsoever.

£100 billion Trident's going to cost us. We can't even fire them unless the Yanks say it's OK – they own the satellites that guide the missiles – so much for 'independent nuclear deterrent'. Russia ain't gonna bomb us – the prevailing wind's from the South West in this country, one of the few things I remember from school. They put a nuke on us and two days later clouds of radioactive shit are floating over Moscow. Who else is going to nuke us? Terrorists? Well, it seems to me a little over the top to employ a £100 billion nuclear missile system to retaliate against a bloke's bedsit in Hackney. I know geezers who will do it over for a fraction of that price.

We need to take a moral lead, trying to convert our arms industry into something more positive. We make billions from arms and some of the places them arms end up reflect very badly on us. Think what could happen if we turned all that brainpower and investment into something creative. We need a government that takes the lead in this.

Next on the list? We should charge them who caused the financial mess in the first place. Instead of giving the banks money, take it off them.

As it is, we're just doing more of the same, giving money to the people who fucked it up in the hope they'll get us out of it. If you're a bus driver and you stick it through the front of a shop window then they don't give you another bus. They tell you to hop it.

The ministers will still be racking up their £500,000 limo bills, like Eric Pickles. Jesus, if ever a man needed to get on a bike.

Surely there's a better system we can move to, one that doesn't involve ripping off people like you and me to pay debts we didn't run up and smashing up the services that make this country great. Change would be hard but it's not like we're in for an easy ride anyway. The government is borrowing at massive levels and, believe me, if it comes down to it, it won't be them and people like them who end up paying it back – it'll be me and you, either in hugely increased taxes, through inflation or by whatever other sneaky means the slags come up with. The ministers will still be racking up their £500,000 limo bills, like Eric Pickles. Jesus, if ever a man needed to get on a bike.

I am not an economist, just a mug shouting at the TV, really. But I do know how this stuff feels on the sharp end. I don't believe that there are no alternatives to the way we do things now, where the country's run just for the benefit of the very rich. I'm not the bloke to come up with them, I'm just an actor. But there has to be something, maybe through the internet because that's got unknown potential, maybe some boffin in some university somewhere has an idea.

Will it ever happen? Not while we keep electing people from the same class. What real interest have they got in changing things? How is George Osborne meant to relate to my mum? But there he goes, with his ten per cent pay rise, selling the banks back to his mates in the City at a knock-down price. I tell you this, if you or I tried that sort of scam we'd have the Old Bill round our door.

As I said, I ain't got time for Miliband but I did think he got shafted at the last election, made to look a bacon-sandwich-dropping slice.

There's a whole media devoted to making sure the same people remain in control. In fact it's so success-ful that people don't question it. It's like when the crash happened. All the news channels were interviewing these geezers from the City saying, 'It's the end of the world.' Why weren't they going out finding other people who were saying, 'Let's lock up these crooks and let them pay their own debts'? All I saw were City Boys saying how terrible it was they wouldn't be getting their bonuses and how they'd all fuck off to Hong Kong if we tried to put any limits on them. Allow me to drive you to Heathrow, you slags.

We were told it was a crisis and needed immediate action. You say we need immediate action on, say, poverty or climate change and they'll tell you, 'We'd love to help but there ain't no money.' There was plenty of money when the rich people looked like suffering weren't there? The TV channels don't report that. They just stick on some bloke who calls himself an analyst who says, 'I have analysed it and I am shafted unless I get a fat wodge of taxpayers' cash, the like of which would make White Dee off *Benefits Street* die of embarrassment to claim. So deliver it in used tenners, I've got a fleet of lorries out the back waiting to take it away. Lovely.'

There was an alternative in Iceland – the country, not the shop – wasn't there? They sacked the government, put the bankers in prison and wrote off people's debts. No chance of that happening here because the media – and the super rich they serve – won't even let people see that's possible. It has us by the nuts. It's

34

My perfect weekend is me in me throne, me command centre. Except I ain't actually issuing any commands.

I am not really what you call a 'driven' person, unless I've been out and had a couple, in which case I will ditch the motor and get a cab back. So my days off tend to focus very strongly on doing nothing. At all.

When I say 'nothing', I have to break it to you now that the life of an actor is not all glamour. I mean I like lying on the settee with a fag, drinking strong coffee, having a snooze and watching shit TV.

We've got a massive flatscreen in our house and it's like having your own personal cinema, except the only slag texting in there is you. I swear, it's so big you could fall through it and find yourself the other side, running around with Sly Stallone in *Rambo*.

Weekdays tend to be really busy with filming so my ideal weekend would involve mainly sleep. I do love me kip. I've always loved my kip. I've never liked getting up early – even though I've had to do it for a few years now, I'll never get used to it. My motto is:

'The early bird that catches the worm: get back in your fucking nest, you feathery little slag.'

I would never want to get up in the morning, given the choice. On a weekend I'll lie in until 10 if Jo allows it. She allows it most times.

I get up and go down. I've never been a breakfast man, just a cup of coffee, pony and a fag. Or rather, a cup of coffee, fag and a pony, get rid of yesterday.

I like to spend as much time as I can with the kids. I'm a bit limited as to what I can do with them because of who I am. I'd like to be out and about taking them more places but it always turns into a bit of a scrum with people following us about so I tend to stay in.

I've got a garden with swings and all that, so we normally just stay round the house playing with them. Sometimes I take Sunnie horse riding. She's very good on a horse, although he's about a hundred, old George.

I always feel a bit inadequate if ever I see these 'day in a life' things in the paper because what I like to do is just fuck all, really. I'm very good at doing absolutely fuck all and I enjoy it.

You read these people saying they sit shelling peas from their garden or painting landscapes, taking the kids fishing and hiring a pedalo, all that shit, but I don't believe 'em. They're on the settee watching *Football Focus* with the rest of us, I reckon.

They should bring the wrestling back, I used to like a bit of that. Haystacks, Big Daddy, the grannies in the front row swearing at the ref. It wasn't highbrow entertainment but it had its place.

Sometimes, I will be forced to go shopping because I have nothing to wear. I put this off for as long as possible because I hate shopping. Really hate it. I just go in one shop, buy a load of stuff at one go, ram it in a hold-all, shove it in the back of the motor and I'm done.

That's rare, though. Mostly I just stay on the settee. If I do need a packet of fags then Jo or Dani will normally nip out to the shops for me so I can stay almost entirely immobile.

I don't do lunch either, just survive on fags and coffee in front of the TV. Sometimes Jo will run round the corner and get us a nice crusty roll but most of the time I have nothing. I like watching the snooker if it's on. I went to the snooker the other day and loved it. I saw John Virgo there, legend. He must miss *Big Break*. He could do with a comb through his hair, I'll say that. He's got a face that looks 'lived in' – by squatters.

Come tea time I like to be watching Rick Stein's *Mediterranean Escapes* or something like that – something about food to go with me dinner. I like Rick Stein, he's got something about him, a bit of passion. It's good to watch someone who's that engaged with life and full of energy when you're spending your fifth hour on the settee, it's like he's doing the running around for ya.

Jo will knock us up an enormous platter plate at tea time. People who come round our house can't believe it – it's a proper platter plate. I have fifty spuds, I've been known to have twelve minted lamb cutlets, I love a rib, three packs with lemon and pepper.

I eat like a snake, I suppose, massive amounts at one go and then nothing for ages.

That's my favourite part of the day, dinner, and then getting back on that settee and catching up with the week's TV. I'm still seeing the family, they're always there, coming in and out or whatever. Jo will nip out and I'll look after Arty or Sunnie. Dani will come in and we'll have a chat. It's like I'm there on me throne, the command centre,

> *I've gone a bit on to the ales and bitters as I've got older. I love 'em but I wonder where it stops. What next? Folk music? Rugby? It could all go very wrong.*

except I ain't actually issuing any commands. Maybe 'be quiet' during an interesting bit of *Antiques Roadshow*. I hate it if they make me miss the price, even though you can rewind nowadays.

I stay up as late as possible, have a couple of lagers. Dani bought me a beer selection from all around the world, all different ales. I chuck 'em in the freezer until they're nearly frozen and then have them. Lovely.

I've gone a bit on to the ales and bitters as I've got older. I love 'em but I wonder where it stops. What next? Folk music? Rugby? It could all go very wrong. Maybe I'll join the Campaign for Real Ale, become a CAMRA man, a dirty great big Six Nations fan and, every time I go in a pub I'll ask the barwoman to refer me to the guest specials on the blackboard. It's only a short step from there to having your own pewter mug, there's the worry.

Back in the day, of course, I would have gone on a three-day bender the whole weekend, just shirked away from any responsibility whatsoever. As I get older that has to change. I want to be around the family a lot more.

I do it less and less because we have Vic Mondays – we do all the filming in The Vic on Monday. That can go over twelve episodes and if you've ripped the arse out of it on the Friday night you won't be on your game and it will show. You're meant to be running the pub, not looking like you're standing on the other side of the bar.

Once I do get into bed, I can never sleep – probably due to the fact I've spent the entire day on my bottle. I watch the TV with the subtitles on so as not to disturb Jo and just drift off. I very often watch the Parliament Channel because it's so boring that it's bound to send you to sleep. I like a nice committee to really get me to drop off. I know a lot of people do the poker and all that but I can't stand it. I like playing poker but I don't want to watch other people playing cards. It's not my idea of a spectator sport.

Eventually sleep comes, maybe before dawn, maybe just after. Sunday will be very much like Saturday, with slightly different TV and I'll probably go to bed earlier because I have to work on the Monday.

And that's it. I like to think this lifestyle prepares me for life if my career would stop tomorrow, God forbid. What would I do? Probably exactly the same, only all week. I think the transition would be quite smooth.

Glossary of Cockney Slang in the Book

Rhyming Slang

Alderman's: Alderman's nail – tail

Apples: Apples and pears – stairs

Boat: Boat race – face

Bottle: Bottle and glass – arse

Brady: Brady bunch – lunch

Brass: Brass door/brass flute – whore/prostitute

Bromleys: Bromley-by-Bows – toes

Bubble: Bubble bath – laugh

Bunny: As in rabbit and pork – talk

China: China plate – mate

Cockle: Cockle and hen – ten

Derby: Derby Kelly – belly (as immortalized in the song 'Boiled Beef and Carrots')

Godiva: Lady Godiva – fiver

Gregory: Gregory peck – neck

Haddock: Haddock and bloater – motor (car)

Khyber: Khyber Pass – arse

Laurel and Hardy – Bacardi

Mince Pies – Eyes

Oliver: Oliver Twist – wrist

Plates: Plates of meat – feet

Pony: Pony and trap – crap

Scotch: Scotch eggs – legs

Sherbert: Sherbert dab – cab

Syrup: Syrup of figs – wig

. . . Danny Dyer

Thrupennies: Thrupenny bits – tits

Treacle: Treacle tart – sweetheart (used as a term for a woman)

Non-Rhyming Slang

Bag of Sand – £1,000

Cannister – head

Melt – idiot

Monkey – £500

Old Bill – police

Pipe – look

Score/apple core/small horse/pony – £25

Slice – not the full loaf. A bit of an idiot

Swede – head

Ton/long'un – £100

Cockney Phrase Book:
How to Communicate on
Your East London Holiday

Posh English: 'Taxi! I wish to be conveyed to Chelsea. Will it cost me under £25?'
Cockney: 'Sherbert! Ere, can I gerrup London for a pony?'
Sherbert: Sherbert dab – cab
Pony here means £25 and should not be confused with 'pony and trap', for crap as the width of London is a bit of a stretch when you're after 'letting go of yesterday' in a hurry.

Posh English: 'That's rather expensive.'
Cockney: 'Yougottabewindingmeupaintcha?'

Posh English: 'Could you lend me ten English pounds?'
Cockney: 'Bung us a cockle mate, could ya?'
Cockle and hen – ten

Posh English: 'You owe me five pounds.'
Cockney: 'Where's me Lady?'
Lady: Lady Godiva – fiver

Posh English: 'I need to use the gentleman's facilities.'
Cockney: 'I'm off for an eyelash.'
  Eyelash – slash

Posh English: 'It's rather cold in here.'
Cockney: 'Bit taters in here mate!'
  Taters: potatoes in the mould – cold

Posh English: 'I have had a fight with the police and need a new suit to appear in court.'
Cockney: 'I've had a tear-up with the Old Bill and need to sort meself a new whistle to see the beak.'
  Old Bill – police
  Whistle: whistle and flute, suit
  Beak – judge or magistrate

Posh English: 'Is that a gun in your pocket or are you just pleased to see me?'
Cockney: 'Is that a shooter in your sky?'
  Shooter – gun
  Sky: Sky rocket – pocket

Posh English: 'There is a tide in the affairs of men, which taken at the flood, leads on to fortune. Omitted, all the voyage of their life is bound in shallows and in miseries. On such a full sea are we now afloat. And we must take the current when it serves, or lose our ventures.'

Cockney: 'Grab it by the Alberts, my saaahhhn!'
Alberts: Albert Halls – balls

Posh English: 'I wish to have a party, would you make the arrangements?'
Cockney: 'I might have a Russell tonight. Make sure you bring some booze.'
Russell: Russell Harty – party

Posh English: 'My husband has requested me to follow the van without delay.'
Cockney: 'My old man said follow the van, and don't dilly dally on the way.'

Posh English: 'I find the Community Police officers to be less reliable than the traditional police.'
Cockney: 'You can't trust a special like your old-time copper.'

Posh English: 'I am gripped by homosexual lust and am willing to engage virtually anyone in sexual congress. You look attractive to me, from head to toe. I particularly admire your new hat and your vintage neckwear, hallmarks of the homosexual community. However, from your unfashionable watch, I see you are not gay.'
Cockney:
  'Any old iron, any old iron, any, any, any, old iron?
  You look neat – talk about a treat,

You look a dapper from your knapper to your feet.
Dressed in style, with a brand new tile,
With your father's old green tie on.
But I wouldn't give you tuppence for your old
    watch chain
Old iron, old iron.

Iron: Iron hoof – poof

Posh English: 'Would you care to come and woo me in a Hampstead gastropub? Nah, nah, nah, nah, nah!'
Cockney: 'Come and make eyes at me, down at the old Bull and Bush. Nah, nah, nah, nah, nah!'

Posh English: 'I find that the more vocal traditional heating ventilation cleaning operatives live lives of unsurpassed joy.'
Cockney: 'Nowhere is there a more 'appier crew, Than them wot sings, "Chim chim cher-ee, chim cher-oo!"'

Acknowledgements

Big thank you to Mark Barrowcliffe for again having to sit there and listening to me bang on. Thank you to Jane for coming up with this nutty idea and to the rest of the Quercus lot for helping get me book out there. Thanks to Denee for standing by me through the tough times and to my family at *EastEnders* for accepting me and embracing all of me. Thanks to my children for making me the man I am today. And to Jo, the only girl I'll ever love.

Index